NEW BY THE

Spirit

To order additional copies of
New by the Spirit, by Arnold Valentin Wallenkampf,
call 1-800-765-6955.

Visit us at **www.reviewandherald.com** for information
on other Review and Herald Products.

NEW BY THE Spirit

*Experiencing the
Life-changing Power
of the Comforter*

ARNOLD VALENTIN WALLENKAMPF

REVIEW AND HERALD® PUBLISHING ASSOCIATION
HAGERSTOWN, MD 21741

The author assumes full responsibility for the accuracy of all facts and quotations as cited in this book.

Unless otherwise indicated, texts of Scripture quoted in this book are from the Revised Standard Version of the Bible, copyright © 1946, 1952, 1971 by the Division of Christian Education of the National Council of the Churches of Christ in the U.S.A. Used by permission.
Texts credited to NEB are from *The New English Bible*. Copyright © The Delegates of the Oxford University Press and the Syndics of the Cambridge University Press 1961, 1970. Reprinted by permission.
Bible texts credited to Phillips are from J. B. Phillips: *The New Testament in Modern English,* Revised Edition. Copyright © J. B. Phillips 1958, 1960, 1972. Used by permission of Macmillan Publishing Co.
Bible texts credited to TEV are from the *Good News Bible*—Old Testament: Copyright © American Bible Society 1976, 1992; New Testament: Copyright © American Bible Society 1966, 1971, 1976, 1992.

This book was
Cover designed by Tina M. Ivany
Cover image © Lars Justinen / GoodSalt.com
Typeset: 11/13 Bembo

PRINTED IN U.S.A.

10 09 08 07 06   5 4 3 2 1

R&H Cataloging Service
Wallenkampf, Arnold Valentin, 1913-1998.
    New by the Spirit

    1. Holy Spirit.   2. Gifts, Spiritual.   I. Title.

                        231.3

ISBN 978-0-8280-1937-8

Dedication

*Dedicated to my former students
at the Seventh-day Adventist Theological Seminary (Far East)*

Contents

CHAPTER 1

The Personhood and Deity of the Spirit

What or Who is the Holy Spirit?

In the King James Version He is often called the Holy Ghost. But what is a ghost? Some ephemeral or floating entity than can be neither located nor easily identified? Without a doubt the designation of the Third Person of the Godhead as "Holy Ghost" has helped to blur or even nullify the acceptance of Him as a person in the thinking of many people. In modern Bible versions He is simply called the Spirit or the Holy Spirit. This makes the Spirit a little less nebulous.

But is it of any importance for us as Christians to learn who or what the Holy Spirit is? Some may maintain that it does not matter whether one knows the Spirit as a Person or as some other entity or even as a mere influence.

But if the Spirit is a mere influence or power, we may try to obtain it or get more of it; we may desire the Spirit in order to use it. Then we hardly stand above pagan animists with their belief in spirit powers. Some may also be filled with pride since they think they have the Spirit while others who do not possess the Spirit to the same extent may be regarded as second rate Christians or not Christians at all.

If, on the other hand, the Spirit is a Person, and part of the Triune God, He deserves worship. Then it becomes important for us that we surrender to Him, as to a person, in love and confidence to be directed by Him, rather than our trying to obtain and use Him. Not knowing the Spirit as a divine Person is a source of prolific error, misconception, sickly enthusiasm, false zeal, and fanaticism.

Theoretically we may all ascribe personality to the Spirit, as we sing "Praise Father, Son, and Holy Ghost," or when we sing the words of the Gloria Patri: "Glory be to the Father, and to the Son, and to the Holy Ghost."

In order to come into a right relationship to the Holy Spirit and to understand His work, it is essential, we believe, that we rightly learn to know the Holy Spirit. The knowledge of the doctrine of the personality of the Spirit is not only fundamental; it is also vital and immeasurably practical. Anyone who knows God the Father and God the Son, but has not attained to the belief in the Spirit as a Person and as God, is not a Christian any more than are those who do not believe in the deity of the Son. Jesus spoke repeatedly of the Spirit as His successor and representative on earth.

What does the Bible tell us about the Spirit? Or how does the Bible present Him?

In the Bible the Spirit or the Holy Spirit is mentioned over 300 times. About 100 times in the Old Testament and well over 200 times in the New. The first mention of the Spirit occurs at the very beginning of the Creation story in Genesis 1. The last mention of Him is in the very last chapter of the Bible, in Revelation 22, only five verses from the end of the entire Bible. In these verses and passages the Bible presents the Spirit as having a mind. Romans 8:27 says, "He who searches the hearts of men knows what is the mind of the Spirit." Having a mind, the Spirit also possesses knowledge. "For what man knoweth the things of a man, save the spirit of man which is in him? even so the things of God knoweth no man, but the Spirit of God" (1 Cor. 2:11, KJV). In addition to mind and knowledge, He has a will: "The same Spirit, who apportions to each one individually as he wills" (1 Cor. 12:11).

Too often we are prone to equate a body with a person. But a physically alive body does not necessarily constitute a functional person. A few years ago I visited a woman whose brain had ceased to function. This particular individual was nearly 100 years old. Her heart was perfect. Her body was strong, but her mind had ceased its normal activity. She knew nothing. She did not recognize my wife Mae and me, although she had known us well. Being without a mind with knowledge, she must be constantly babied. She never regained the powers of her mind. She was a mere entity, not a functional person, although she possessed a healthy body. This grandmother had ceased to be a person in any real sense. She died as a nonperson.

The primary requisites for being a person are to possess a mind with knowledge and a will. The texts just quoted show that the Spirit has all three. The Spirit consequently is a Person although devoid of a body.

The Spirit is a Person who loves. Paul implores the church members at Rome "by our Lord Jesus Christ and by the love of the Spirit," to pray for him (Rom. 15:30). Only a person can love. The Father is a Person, and He loves us (see John 3:16); the Son is a Person, and He loves us (see John

13:1). As a Person, the Spirit also loves us.

Being a Person, the Spirit is capable of personal feelings. Isaiah tells us that the Israelites "rebelled and grieved his holy Spirit." Isaiah 63:10. It is impossible for you to grieve your car or your lawn mower. Neither can you grieve a tree. You cannot make them feel sorry. Nor can you grieve or make an influence feel sorry or grieved. Grieve is a love word. Only a person who loves can be grieved. The Spirit possesses feelings and can be grieved. Hence, this is further evidence that He is a Person. The apostle Paul admonishes the Ephesian believers not to follow the example of the ancient Israelites and "grieve the Holy Spirit of God" (Eph. 4:30; see Heb. 3: 9-12).

Jointly the Three Persons in the Trinity seek man as a lost sheep and offer him salvation. In unison They engage in his rescue. Together and separately They invite us to salvation (see Isa. 1:18; Pro. 23:26; Matt. 11:28; Heb. 3:7, 8; Rev. 22:17).

As God is good, so the Spirit is good. The psalmist speaks of the good Spirit (see Ps. 143:10), and Nehemiah says that God gave the Israelites His "good Spirit to instruct them" (Neh. 9:20). These texts again point up the personality of the Spirit.

In speaking to the students at Avondale College back in 1899 Ellen G. White emphasized the personhood of the Spirit when she said, "We need to realize that the Holy Spirit, who is as much a person as God is a person, is walking through these grounds."[1]

Another evidence that the Spirit is a Person is that the New Testament writers, in recording the words of Jesus, used the masculine pronoun *ekeinos* (he), although the word "Spirit" is a neuter noun in the Greek language as it is in English. "When the Counselor comes, whom I shall send to you from the Father, even the Spirit of truth, who proceeds from the Father, he will bear witness to me" (John 15:26). This is done repeatedly. "When the Spirit of truth comes, he will guide you into all the truth; for he will not speak on his own authority, but whatever he hears he will speak, and he will declare to you the things that are to come. He will glorify me, for he will take what is mine and declare it to you" (John 16:13, 14). The Spirit also refers to Himself by using the first person pronoun "me" in Acts 13:2.

In spite of all these evidences that the Spirit is a Person, He is often thought of and spoken of as an "it." The neuter gender for Spirit, both in the original Greek and in English, has undoubtedly contributed to this concept. So also have probably the many symbols or emblems used in the Bible to present Him, His nature, and His operations. Some of these are fire, wind, oil, seal, and others which will be discussed in a later chapter.

All of these contribute to the concept of thinking of the Spirit as a non-person, even in Christian thinking, although He is One of the Three Persons in the Godhead. It is He who reminds us that we are the children of God. "The Holy Spirit has a personality, else He could not bear witness to our spirits and with our spirits that we are the children of God."[2]

"The Holy Spirit is not a mere spirit. . . . Christ gives Him names which are personal names or indicate and name a distinct Person. He calls Him the Comforter, for example. He also mentions personal works, as, for example, when He declares that He will bear witness of Christ. Then He says: 'He will teach you all things.'"[3]

Has it ever occurred to you, that as you thank the Father and the Son for your salvation, you should also thank the Spirit for your redemption? The Father gave His Son, and Jesus paid our redemption price on Calvary. But if it had not been for the love of the Spirit and His willingness to come here and effectualize in us the objective salvation, wrought for us by Jesus on the cross, we would still be irretrievably lost, despite Christ's sacrifice.

The Spirit, being a Person, should not be treated as a power which we should try to get hold of in order to use. Rather, we should regard and treat Him as a divine Person, whom we should not try to use according to our wills. We should permit Him to direct us and use us according to His will.

The Deity of the Spirit

God is a trinity. He is made up of three persons: The Father, the Son, and the Holy Spirit. GOD is the divine family name. As we as individuals belong to a certain family and carry a family name, so God has a family name. This name is GOD. As we as individuals in our respective families have individual or personal names, in addition to our family name, so each person in the Godhead, the Trinity, has an individual name. These are the Father, the Son, and the Holy Spirit.

Although God is made up of Three Persons, we say that God is one, and we call ourselves monotheists. We feel justified in doing this because the three persons in the Godhead are one in purpose, thought, will, plans and intentions. To us as human beings this appears perplexing and impossible. We think of different persons as having different wills, thoughts, purposes, and plans. This is true even when the relationships are most close and intimate. But God is different. He is one in Three Persons.

"There are three living persons of the heavenly trio . . . the Father, the Son, and the Holy Spirit."[4] With the ancient Hebrews, Seventh-day Adventists and other Christians aver: "The Lord our God is one Lord"

(Deut. 6:4). Moses in speaking of God says "our God." In this text "our God" could more correctly be translated by the plural "our Gods." Even with their intense monotheism, the Jews still used a plural name for God. Rather than attribute this usage to the *pluralis majestatis* (plural of majesty), it is logical to deduce that Moses used the plural name for God because there is a plurality of persons in the Godhead—the Father, the Son, and the Spirit.

The Holy Spirit, one of the Three Persons in the Godhead, is often mentioned in the Bible. In the very opening words of the Bible, the Spirit is introduced in the Creation narrative. "In the beginning God created the heavens and the earth. The earth was without form and void, and darkness was upon the face of the deep; and the Spirit of God was moving over the face of the waters" (Gen. 1:1, 2).

It is by His creative power that God is singled out and set apart from the idols. When a distinction is made between the idols and the true God, the power of creation is repeatedly referred to as the litmus test identifying the true God—the Creator. "All the gods of the people are idols; but the Lord made the heavens" (Ps. 96:5; see also Jer. 10:1-16). The Father's agent in Creation was Jesus Christ. "All things were made through him, and without him was not anything made that was made" (John 1:3).

creativity The Spirit was present and actively associated with God the Father and God the Son in Creation. Speaking of Creation, the psalmist exclaims, "When thou sendest forth thy Spirit, they are created; and thou renewest the face of the ground" (Ps. 104:30). The book of Job echoes the creatorship of the Spirit: "The spirit of God has made me, and the breath of the Almighty gives me life" (Job 33:4).

All the Three Persons in the Trinity were united in the work of Creation. What the members of the Godhead do, They do together as a unit, although Their particular activities or tasks may be different. Being a partner in Creation proves the Spirit's divinity.

Baptism is a symbolic portal leading into the church. Through baptism the believer becomes a member of the heavenly family as he is baptized "in [into] the name of the Father and of the Son and of the Holy Spirit" (Matt. 28:19). "To all who received him, who believed in his name, he gave power to become children of God" (John 1:12). Through this symbolic rite, to which the believer has been prompted to submit by the love of the Father, and through the ministry of the—Spirit, he has left his old family and become a member of the family of God. He is now a brother of Jesus, who will impart to the believer His grace or power to live according to the divine will.|The Spirit is from now on to be his constant companion to succor him in his warfare against sinful promptings from within his own being and enticements from without. This is in keeping with the thinking of Paul as he expresses it in 2 Cor. 13:14: "The grace of the Lord Jesus Christ and the love of God and the fellowship of the Holy Spirit be with you all." Together with Matthew 28:19 this verse provides the most complete and explicit summary of the doctrine of the Trinity.

Jointly the Three Persons of the Deity work for the salvation of man. "The Father, the Son, and the Holy Spirit, the three holy dignitaries of heaven, have declared that they will strengthen men to overcome the powers of darkness. All the facilities of heaven are pledged to those who by their baptismal vows have entered into a covenant with God."[5]

By both Jews and Muslims, Christians have often been, and still are, accused of being polytheists, or worshippers of more than one God. As Christians we admit there are Three Persons in the Godhead, but since they are one in purpose, in mind, in character, but not in person, we still reckon ourselves to be monotheists. The Christian God—three in one—is completely different from the gods in the Olympic heaven and in the Nordic sagas. In both those places constant and perennial warfare raged among the different gods. Those gods each had their individual will and plan and were definitely not one in purpose and mind. The Christian God, on the other hand, is not a triad of gods, but one God in three—a trinity.

The apostle Peter, in speaking to Ananias, equated God and the Spirit by referring to them interchangeably. "Peter said, 'Ananias, why has Satan filled your heart to lie to the Holy Spirit and to keep back part of the proceeds of the land? While it remained unsold, did it not remain your own? And after it was sold, was it not at your disposal? How is it that you have contrived this deed in your heart? You have not lied to men but to God" (Acts 5:3, 4). This interchange forcibly emphasizes the unity that exists among the persons in the Godhead (see also Acts 10:38).

But Peter is not the only Bible writer who interchanges the names of God and the Spirit; Paul does the same. To the Cor. he writes: "Now there are varieties of gifts, but the same Spirit; and there are varieties of service, but the same Lord; and there are varieties of working, but it is the same God who inspires them all in every one. To each is given the manifestation of the Spirit for the common good. To one is given through the Spirit the utterance of wisdom, and to another the utterance of knowledge according to the same Spirit." "All these are inspired by one and the same Spirit, who apportions to each one individually as he wills." "And God has appointed in the church first apostles, second prophets, third teachers, then workers of miracles, then healers, helpers, administrators, speakers in various kinds of tongues" (1 Cor. 12:4-8, 11, 28). In this passage Paul uses the Spirit, Lord, and God interchangeably.

At Creation God designed that man was to be the Spirit's dwelling place on earth. The Spirit is life, and part of that life God wanted to abide within man. "From eternal ages it was God's purpose that every created being, from the bright and holy seraph to man, should be a temple for the indwelling of the Creator. Because of sin, humanity ceased to be a temple for God. . . . They [the Jews in Christ's time] did not yield themselves as holy temples for the Divine Spirit."[6] This last statement is true for anyone who rejects God's plan.

Thus sin disrupted God's plan. But through the new birth God's plan is again fulfilled. "Do you not know that you are God's temple and that God's Spirit dwells in you?" (1 Cor. 3:16). "Do you not know that your body is a temple of the Holy Spirit within you, which you have from God?" (1 Cor. 6:19).

Calvin says: "Nor, indeed, does Scripture in speaking of Him [the Spirit] refrain from the designation 'God.' For Paul concludes that we are the temple of God from the fact that his Spirit dwells in us. . . . The apostle himself sometimes writes that 'we are God's temple,' at other times in the same sense, 'the temple of the Holy Spirit.'"[7]

Through the Spirit, God in person desires to live within man. Luther says, "The Holy Spirit is not a mere spirit—a creature, for example, or something apart from God and yet given to man by Him, or merely the work of God which He performs in our hearts but that He is a Spirit who Himself is God in essence."[8]

Jesus, in announcing the Spirit's coming to the disciples, called Him *another* Counselor ("Comforter," KJV) in John 14:16. He says that God will send this Counselor because "I will *pray* the Father." In this passage Jesus is addressing His Father as an equal. The verb Jesus used for "pray" in this passage has the basic meaning of "to ask" or "to enquire." In John's writings it usually connotes an individual asking something from a peer.[9] Jesus is here addressing His Father as an equal in petitioning a gift for His followers.

Jesus intended to send someone to the disciples, and succeeding generations of His followers, who is like Himself—divine. Jesus had previously equated Himself with His Father. Now He likens Himself to the Spirit. Consequently, They are all alike—divine.

The attributes ascribed to the Spirit in the Bible are also the same as those credited to God. The Spirit possesses life (Rom. 8:2); He is omniscient (1 Cor. 2:10, 11); He is omnipresent (Ps. 139: 1-6); He is omnipotent (Gen. 1:2); He is holy (Luke 11:13); He is eternal (Heb. 9:14). Many more attributes could be enumerated showing that the Spirit is God, for these attributes are not communicated to a creature. These therefore further show that the Spirit is divine.

But theoretical knowledge about the Spirit is not sufficient.

What really matters is how I think of the Spirit, and how I relate to Him as a Person during the hours of daily life and personal decision making. Do I in daily life act as if He is a Person who can be constantly by my side, guide me in my thinking, enable me to reach right conclusions and arrive at the most valid decisions? Do I believe I may have a constant, divine guide and helper at my side? The promise is ours: "Provision is made by God Himself for every soul that turns to the Lord, to receive His immediate cooperation. The Holy Spirit becomes His efficiency."[10]

---

[1] Ellen G. White, *Evangelism* (Washington, D.C.: Review and Herald Pub. Assn., 1946), p. 616.

[2] *Ibid.,* p. 617.

[3] From Martin Luther's sermon on John 15:26,27 in *Luther's Works* (Saint Louis, Mo.: Concordia Publishing House, 1964), vol. 24, p. 297.

[4] Ellen G. White, *Evangelism,* p. 615.

[5] Ellen G. White Comments, *Seventh-day Adventist Bible Commentary* (Washington, D.C.: Review and Herald Pub. Assn., 1953, 1957), vol. 5, p. 1110.

[6] Ellen G. White, *The Desire of Ages* (Mountain View, Calif.: Pacific Press Pub. Assn., 1940), p. 161.

[7] John Calvin, *Institutes,* bk. I, ch. 13, par. 15.

[8] Martin Luther's sermon on John 15:26, 27 in *Luther's Works,* vol. 24, p. 297.

[9] Campbell Morgan, *The Spirit of God* (Old Tappan, N.J.: Fleming H. Revell Co., 1973), pp. 108, 109.

[10] Ellen G. White, *My Life Today* (Washington, D.C.: Review and Herald Pub. Assn., 1952), p. 47.

CHAPTER 2

Symbols of the Holy Spirit

In studying about the Holy Spirit or trying to get acquainted with Him, as He is presented in the Bible, no one should neglect the symbols, emblems, types, or illustrations used for Him in the Scriptures. A few of these symbols or emblems of the Spirit will be discussed in this chapter.

Only through an acquaintance with the different symbols and varied emblems used for the Holy Spirit in the Bible can His work and ministry in the believer's life be adequately understood. Only in this way will we be able to grasp His position and understand the work He desires to do in your life and mine. The types used for the Spirit in the Scriptures serve to emphasize and illustrate teachings and ministries that might otherwise be difficult or even impossible to understand.

For us as followers of God it is essential to understand and know the work of the Spirit, since through His ministry we are transformed and fitted for heavenly society. We have no inherent holiness. We can become and remain holy only as we are possessed by the Spirit. As the holy anointing oil made everything it touched holy (see Lev. 8:10-12, 30), so the Spirit is the One who makes us holy. We are holy in His holiness, loving in His love, strong in His strength, tender in His tenderness, patient in His patience, calm in His peace, and consecrated in His consecration. "Through the agency of the Holy Spirit, the soul is enlightened, and the character is renewed, sanctified, and uplifted."[1] If we get out of touch with Him by neglecting prayer, the fragrance of His presence will be wanting in our lives.

The direction of the church since the ascension of Jesus has been under the administration of the Holy Spirit. The Holy Spirit is God's intended vicegerent of Jesus Christ on this earth. He is to administer His church by endeavoring to perfect in its members the image of our Lord and Savior. It is with the Holy Spirit that you and I are to be intimately associated in our transformation of character into the likeness of our Creator.

Inasmuch as we are going to work with the Holy Spirit, it behooves us to try acquainting ourselves with Him and His character and learning to understand Him and His way of working in us. This we can do more adequately as we understand also the symbols under which He is presented in the Scriptures.

Ambassador. One symbol of the Spirit is an ambassador. The Holy Spirit is God's ambassador to man in sin and rebellion; He has the task of trying to restore man's loyalty to His Creator and God. After his great sin David prayed, "Take not thy holy Spirit from me" (Ps. 51:11). When nations get into strained relations one with another, and before they declare war, they withdraw their ambassadors. The essence of this prayer, after David had hurt God by his gruesome sins of adultery and murder, was, "Please, God, don't take Your Ambassador away from me, but leave Him so that I may have a chance to speak to You through Him and come back into a friendly relationship with You."

Eyes. Another symbol of the Holy Spirit, presented in Revelation 5:6 is eyes. The seven eyes mentioned are said to be the seven spirits of God. The number seven indicates completeness and is symbolic.

The seven eyes signify the all-sufficiency of the Spirit. As the eye of God, the ministry of the Holy Spirit is complete and perfect, possessing insight, foresight, and hindsight. These are gifts of God through the Spirit.

The prophet Elisha received hindsight when his servant, Gehazi, came back after overtaking Naaman. In the story in 2 Kings 5:20-27, the servant ran after the Syrian nobleman, Naaman, and told him that his master wanted some gold and some garments for some needy students. Naaman gave the servant both. When Gehazi returned to his master, Elisha asked him where he had been. The servant said, "Nowhere." But Elisha said, "Did I not see you when you ran after Naaman?" I don't know whether Elisha saw him at the time or if God just gave him the hindsight as the servant came into his presence.

Another illustration is Peter in his dealings with Ananias and Sapphira in Acts 5. Ananias came before Peter, and Peter asked him, "For how much did you sell your farm?" Ananias told him that he had sold it for the sum of money he had given to the church. Then Peter said, "Ananias, why has Satan filled your heart to lie to the Holy Spirit and to keep back part of the proceeds of the land?" (Acts 5:3). The Holy Spirit gave Peter hindsight. He told Peter the actual amount which Ananias and Sapphira had received from the sale of their property and of which they were withholding part while pretending to give all. Peter saw into the past through the hindsight the Holy Spirit gave him.

The apostle Paul on his last visit to Jerusalem evidently possessed foresight. Before his arrival in the city he knew of the bonds and afflictions which would befall him. The story is recorded in Acts 20:22, 23. God gave him a glimpse into the future by telling him what would happen to him.

Our perceptivity may also be enhanced through the help of the Spirit. We too may receive insight, foresight, and also hindsight. How perceptive are we? All of us do not have the same perceptivity. There are some people who have very keen perceptivity. This is a gift of God through the Spirit.

You and I may also become more perceptive through the help of the Holy Spirit. "If we are constantly looking unto Jesus and receiving His Spirit, we shall have clear eyesight."[2]

There are times in our experience when we have had a complicated interview. It may have dealt with a spiritual problem or been a business interview or something else. At times we came away from it with the sweet assurance that everything we did and said had been right. But on another occasion in a like experience we felt that nothing we did or said was right. Some of us have had both experiences.

What accounted for the difference? Everything went well when we depended on the Holy Spirit's guidance. It was only when we rushed away in our own wisdom that everything seemed to go wrong. But if we commit ourselves to God to do His work in His way, we may claim this promise from God: "When unconsciously we are in danger of exerting a wrong influence, the angels will be by our side, prompting us to a better course, choosing our words for us, and influencing our actions. Thus our influence may be a silent, unconscious, but mighty power in drawing others to Christ and the heavenly world."[3] We may have clearer eyesight if we avail ourselves of the help of the Holy Spirit.

Part of the Laodicean message says, "Anoint thine eyes with eyesalve, that thou mayest see" (Rev. 3:18, KJV). The eyesalve is the Holy Spirit.

Water. In John 7:37-39 we find the account of Jesus at the Feast of Tabernacles: "On the last day of the feast, the great day, Jesus stood up and proclaimed, 'If any one thirst, let him come to me and drink. He who believes in me, as the scripture has said, "Out of his heart shall flow rivers of living water."' Now this he said about the Spirit."

There is no life without water. Water is essential to life. So there will be no spiritual life, even in a professed believer, without the presence of the Spirit.

19

"The cry of Christ to the thirsty soul is still going forth, and it appeals to us with even greater power than to those who heard it in the temple on the last day of the feast. The fountain is open for all. The weary and exhausted ones are offered the refreshing draught of eternal life. Jesus is still crying, 'If any man thirst, let him come unto Me, and drink.'"[4]

You and I may receive a fuller measure of the Holy Spirit if we want to. Isaiah 44:3 reads: "I will pour water on the thirsty land, and streams on the dry ground; I will pour my Spirit upon your descendants, and my blessing on your offspring." This is Hebrew poetry. In Western poetry we usually have rhyme and meter. The Hebrews had what we call parallelism. First they expressed the thought in one way, and then they paraphrased it, as it were, and expressed the same thought in different words. Hebrew poetry is built on parallelism. This verse consequently says the same thing in two different ways. The second part explains what the first part actually means. The verse indicates that through pouring water on dry ground there will be growth.

One thing that constantly amazed me during the years we lived in southern California was that apparently lifeless and seemingly worthless soil would sprout life with gorgeous flowers by our pouring water on it. It just looked like dead sand—just sand. But by pouring water upon it, we produced a garden of verdure. Apparently there are seeds all through the sand, and when water is poured on it, they start growing. The California desert blooms in the spring; many kinds of flowers will be found—even rare flowers. Then when the months of rain are gone, the ground dries up and again becomes a barren desert.

A parched soul is dead in trespasses and sin—until and unless the Holy Spirit touches it. Then it, too, although barren and dry before like the desert without water, may be filled with life and beauty. There is no life in the desert without water.

The only positive evidence of life is growth! If something is growing, it is alive. If a person starts growing and blossoming like the desert in springtime, then we know that there must be life in him through the Holy Spirit. But if there is no growth, there probably is no life.

In His visit with the Samaritan woman Jesus again used the symbol of water for the Holy Spirit. "Whoever drinks of the water that I shall give him will never thirst; the water that I shall give him will become in him a spring of water welling up to eternal life" (John 4:14).

"The water that Christ referred to was the revelation of His grace in His word; His Spirit, His teaching, is as a satisfying fountain to every soul."[5]

20

Oil, Unction, Eyesalve. In the parable all 10 of the virgins had lamps. Their lamps represent the Word of God, the Bible. But the wise virgins, in addition to the lamps, had oil. Oil, as a prophetic symbol, denotes the Spirit.[6]

I recall that when I was a boy on a farm in Sweden, we used kerosene lanterns in the barn during the winter. The young people of today are very knowledgeable, but there are certain aspects of life about which they hardly know anything. One of them is oil lanterns.

In order for a kerosene lamp to give light, it must have oil. A wick—a piece of cloth—goes from the burner into the oil container. Through this piece of cloth the oil is drawn from the container up to the burner. As one lights the wick, the lantern gives light. If there is no oil, there will be no light. I have had the experience of having the oil run out in our lantern, just as the foolish virgins had their oil run out. Then we had no light.

As Christians we are supposed to be lights. "You are the light of the world," said Jesus. "Let your light so shine before men, that they may see" (Matt. 5:14, 16). Since oil or unction represents the Holy Spirit, we will give no light to the world if the Holy Spirit does not dwell within us.

"You have been anointed by the Holy One, and you all know" (1 John 2:20). "The anointing which you received from him abides in you, and you have no need that any one should teach you; as his anointing teaches you about everything" (verse 27). In the King James Version verse 20 reads: "Ye have an unction from the Holy One, and ye know all things." What is an unction? An anointing? What does the apostle John mean here? He is here speaking about the anointing by the Holy Spirit that will impart to the recipients insight and knowledge.

It is interesting to note that verse 27 reads, "You have no need that any one should teach you." God is anxious to guide each willing follower. "The Lord will teach us our duty just as willingly as He will teach somebody else. If we come to Him in faith, He will speak His mysteries to us personally."[7]

Dove. Possibly one of the most familiar figures of the Spirit is the dove. It is employed as a symbol of the Spirit only once in the Bible. Nevertheless, it is well-known, since this was the representation God gave to the Spirit when He bestowed Him upon Jesus at the time of His baptism. "John bare record, saying, I saw the Spirit descending from heaven like a dove, and it abode upon him" (John 1:32, KJV).

"The Lord had promised to give John a sign whereby he might know who was the Messiah, and now as Jesus went up out of the water, the promised sign was given; for he saw the heavens opened, and the Spirit of God, like a dove of burnished gold, hovered over the head of Christ, and a voice came from heaven, saying, 'This is my beloved Son, in whom I am well pleased.'"[8]

The dove aptly symbolizes the beauty of the Holy Spirit's character. It denotes His purity. Matthew 10:16 speaks of Christ's followers, who ought to be harmless, or still better translated "unmixed" or "pure," as doves. The dove descended from heaven upon Jesus. So purity can be imparted to men only from heaven. This, with charity (or love), is the attribute that God prizes most.[9]

The dove is further a symbol of peace. It is not a scavenger, as the vulture or the raven, relishing carrion; nor is it a bird given to fights. It is a gentle bird. Thus it also symbolizes the gentleness, love, peace, and heavenly origin of the Spirit as He imparts peace of heart and soul to Christ's followers with accompanying gentleness. The dove gently moves upon its eggs until they are hatched. So the Spirit tenderly guards prospective candidates for salvation through life, after having created new life within them from on high, ultimately to usher them into heavenly society. For this He is continuously trying to prepare men and women. Since the Spirit is gentle, He will make His followers gentle. This is part of the fruit of the Spirit (see Gal. 5:23).

The dove (pigeon) has historically often been used as a messenger. The Spirit is God's messenger to men or His ambassador to us from heaven. As a nation maintains ambassadors in other nations in times of peace, so God has His representative—the dove of the Holy Spirit—with men who are not at war with Him. He is constantly presenting to them messages from heaven and trying to transform them to fit into heavenly society.

The dove is constant in love. It is one bird that is said to live in the strictest monogamy, never desiring another mate. The love of the Holy Spirit is likewise constant. The love of the Spirit (see Rom. 15:30) is the spring that tips the scales and brings the converted sinner into the path of obedience. Love starts the sinner on the road heavenward. He is perfect in His love toward us by His constancy of affection. "His love is like *air*, free and pure; like the *sun*, warm and healing; like the *mountains*, strong and protecting; like the *sea*, deep and powerful; like the *stream* which moves the mill-wheel, useful and gladdening; like the *wind*, purifying and helpful; and like the *soil* to the tree, nourishing and productive."[10]

When Jesus said, "Lo, I am with you alway, even unto the end of the world" (Matt. 28:20, KJV), He was referring to the Spirit through whom He was going to be with His followers, for "Christ is to live in His representatives by the spirit of truth."[11]

Seal and Earnest. "Who hath also sealed us, and given the earnest of the Spirit in our hearts" (2 Cor. 1:22, KJV).

When a person by faith accepts Christ, he is immediately sealed by God with the Spirit (see Ephesians 1:13). The Spirit is the seal rather than the sealing agent.

The seal in the Old Testament was a token of ownership (see Jeremiah 32:9, 10). The Spirit in the life of the believer is a sign that he belongs to God. He is also a sign of God's authority in the life of the believer; He alone is to control the child of God. The seal of Rome on the grave of Jesus was evidence to all that only Rome claimed control over the grave (see Matt. 27:64-66).

The seal also guarantees security to the believer. The Spirit is a sign that no one can touch or take the believer out of God's hand or care.

See John 10:27-30. God will never break the seal; He will not go back on what He has promised. So the only being who can break the seal is the believer himself. If he chooses no longer to be God's servant, or to be controlled by God, God will release him. This is in accordance with the free moral choice God has granted to every intelligent being.

The Spirit is more than God's seal of ownership and authority in the believer's life. He is also the pledge, or guarantee, to the believer on the part of God that He will ultimately bring him the full gift of salvation by taking him out of this world of sin and giving him an inheritance in His eternal kingdom (see Eph. 1:13, 14; 2 Cor. 5:5). Even in human affairs the earnest money, or down payment, is the purchaser's pledge that he will go through with a particular transaction. The Spirit is God's down payment on His promised salvation. As the rainbow to Noah was God's guarantee that there would not be another flood, so the Spirit in the life of the believer is the believer's constant reminder of ultimate salvation despite the typhoons of trial along the way (see Eph. 4:30).

Light and Fire. Through His Spirit Jesus reaches everywhere and "lighteth every man that cometh into the world" (John 1:9, KJV). "As the plant receives the sunshine, . . . so are we to receive the Holy Spirit."[12] No form of life can exist without light. So life in one's soul can't exist without the Spirit.

Fire had a significant meaning to people familiar with Old Testament traditions, for it denoted the presence of God (see Ex. 3:2); it also represented the protection of God (see Ex. 13:21), and the approval of God (see Lev. 9:24). John the Baptist said that Jesus would baptize or imbue His followers with the presence of this protecting power (see Matt. 3:11; Mark 1:8).

Fire is also a cleansing agent, but not for straw, stubble, or wood. They will be consumed by fire rather than being cleansed. But metals will be cleansed by fire. Through the Spirit God will try His people as by fire. Today, during probationary time, God through His Spirit is eager to burn away the impurities in our characters. Both Isaiah and Malachi speak of this cleansing process that God's elect will pass through before Jesus returns in His glory (see Isa. 33:14-16; Mal. 3:1-3).

"The prophet Isaiah had declared that the Lord would cleanse His people from their iniquities 'by the spirit of judgment, and by the spirit of burning.' The word of the Lord to Israel was, 'I will turn My hand upon thee, and purely purge away thy dross, and take away all thy tin' (Isa. 4:4; 1:25). To sin, wherever found, 'our God is a consuming fire' (Heb. 12:29). In all who submit to His power the Spirit of God will consume sin. But if men cling to sin, they become identified with it. Then the glory of God, which destroys sin, must destroy them."[13]

Wind. The wind is not visible, nor do we know from where it comes or where it goes. But although invisible, its effects are plainly seen. "Christ uses the wind as a symbol of the Spirit of God. As the wind bloweth whither it listeth, . . . so it is with the Spirit of God. We do not know through whom it will be manifested."[14]

The Spirit is sovereign. Man, or the believer, is not to control the Spirit any more than man is to, or can, control the wind. The wind blows where it pleases.

Jesus said to Nicodemus that man must be born from above (see John 3:7, footnote). The wind, too, is from the heavens above and blows on the earth. Anyone who has had any acquaintance with a tornado, a hurricane, or a typhoon knows the dreadful force or power of wind. The Spirit's work in regeneration is also powerful but not unto destruction, but rather toward rebuilding or regenerating man.

Of the Three Persons in the Godhead the Spirit is the most mysterious, and possibly also the most unfamiliar, even to Christians. Jesus came to reveal or make known the Father (see John 1:18), and man saw Jesus in human form. But no one has ever seen the Spirit, nor has anyone revealed Him to us. It is God's purpose that every follower of His come to know the Spirit as His personal friend and guide through life, and finally through the pearly gates into His eternal kingdom.★

★ Those who are interested in a more complete presentation on biblical symbols of the Spirit may consult F. E. Marsh, *Emblems of the Holy Spirit* (Grand Rapids, Mich.: Kregel

Publications, 1971), and Leslie Hardinge, *Dove of Gold* (Nashville, Tenn.: Southern Pub. Assn., 1972).

---

[1] Ellen G. White, *Selected Messages,* bk. 1 (Washington, D.C.: Review and Herald Pub. Assn., 1958), p. 134.

[2] Ellen G. White, *Selected Messages,* bk. 2, p. 60.

[3] Ellen G. White, *Christ's Object Lessons* (Washington, D.C.: Review and Herald Pub. Assn., 1941), pp. 341, 342.

[4] Ellen G. White, *The Desire of Ages,* p. 454.

[5] Ellen G. White, *Testimonies to Ministers* (Mountain View, Calif.: Pacific Press Pub. Assn., 1923), p. 390.

[6] Ellen G. White, *Christ's Object Lessons,* see p. 407.

[7] Ellen G. White, *The Desire of Ages,* p. 668.

[8] Ellen G. White Comments, *Seventh-day Adventist Bible Commentary,* vol. 5, p. 1078.

[9] "The attributes which God prizes most are charity and purity." Ellen G. White, *Testimonies* (Mountain View, Calif.: Pacific Press Pub. Assn., 1948), vol. 5, p. 85.

[10] F. E. Marsh, *Emblems of the Holy Spirit* (Grand Rapids, Mich.: Kregel Publications, 1971), p. 17.

[11] Ellen G. White, *Review and Herald,* April 4, 1893.

[12] Ellen G. White, *Education* (Mountain View, Calif.: Pacific Press Pub. Assn., 1952), p. 106.

[13] Ellen G. White, *The Desire of Ages,* p. 107.

[14] Ellen G. White, *Selected Messages,* bk. 2, p. 15.

CHAPTER 3

Jesus and the Spirit

During His incarnation Jesus was constantly under the direction of the Spirit. This was true from the very first moment of His life to His expiring breath on the cross.

He was conceived by Mary through the overshadowing power of the Spirit. The angel had said to her, when he invited her to become the mother of the Messiah, "The Holy Spirit will come upon you, and the power of the Most High will overshadow you; therefore the child to be born will be called holy, the Son of God" (Luke 1:35). God prepared a body for Jesus (see Heb. 10:5) through the power of the Spirit that overshadowed Mary. Jesus was born by the Spirit, and the Spirit indwelt Him from birth.

Under the Spirit's guidance Jesus grew and developed as a child "and became strong, filled with wisdom; and the favor of God was upon him" (Luke 2:40). At 12 years of age He accompanied His parents to the Passover feast at Jerusalem and listened to and followed the Spirit's directions as He visited with the Jewish elders in the temple. The Spirit imparted wisdom to Him as He asked questions and answered theirs (see Luke 2:46-49). While there He became aware of His earthly mission.

The next 18 years of His life, embracing His teens and early manhood, are largely hidden from our awareness, but under the Spirit's guidance He "increased in wisdom and in stature, and in favor with God and man" (Luke 2:52). As a youth He worked in the carpenter shop of His human "father," Joseph, and was obedient to His parents (see Luke 2:51).

Jesus emerged from His obscurity at the time of His baptism. He was then ready to enter upon His public ministry. In preparation for that work He was visibly endowed with the abiding presence of the Spirit in the form of a dove (see John 1:32, 33). The prophet Isaiah had foretold that the

Spirit would rest upon the Messiah by saying, "The Spirit of the Lord shall rest upon him, the spirit of wisdom and understanding, the spirit of counsel and might, the spirit of knowledge and the fear of the Lord" (Isa. 11:2).

Jesus received the fullness of the Spirit. John testified to this by saying that "God giveth not the Spirit by measure unto him" (John 3:34, KJV). Jesus was always filled or possessed by the Spirit.

But the infilling of the fullness of the Spirit was not an arbitrary bestowal, ordered by His Father; rather, Jesus chose to remain a temple of the Spirit, as God had originally purposed every person to be. Jesus claimed and welcomed the Spirit's sustaining power. "As a man He supplicated the throne of God, till His humanity was charged with a heavenly current that connected humanity with divinity."[1] Each morning He supplicated His Father for wisdom and strength for that day. The prophet Isaiah, speaking anticipatively for Jesus, says, "The Lord God has given me the tongue of those who are taught, that I may know how to sustain with a word him that is weary. Morning by morning he wakens my ear to hear as those who are taught. The Lord God has opened my ear, and I was not rebellious, I turned not backward" (Isa. 50:4, 5).

Jesus was humble and teachable, not merely willing but anxious to do His Father's will. In the following words the psalmist expresses his attitude: "I delight to do thy will, O my God; thy law is within my heart" (Ps. 40:8).

He was sealed with the Spirit (see John 6:27). The Spirit's sealing was a sign that He fully and wholly belonged to God and was under His direction. No one else but the owner of the seal had the right of access to Him. He was fully committed to His Father's will and way.

Thus His acts were in accordance with His Father's will. He did not go His own way and do "his own thing," as the phrase ran a few years ago. He went His Father's way and did His work (see John 4:34). "From His earliest years He was possessed of one purpose; He lived to bless others."[2] "There was not one selfish act in all his life."[3]

Immediately upon His baptism Jesus was led by the Spirit into the wilderness (see Matt. 4:1). Occasionally we may be prone to think that it was not the Holy Spirit but some other spirit that prompted Jesus to go into the wilderness. But Jesus heeded the promptings of no spirit but the Holy Spirit. Thus the Spirit led Him into the wilderness seclusion to be alone with His Father that He might enjoy His intimate fellowship and gain directives for His mission before entering upon His public ministry.

After Jesus had been alone with His Father for 40 days of fasting and prayer the wily tempter assailed Him. As a man Jesus by that time was weary, hungry and emaciated. In this state Satan assailed Him with the seducing offer of food. With an appeal to the appetite Satan had vanquished Adam and Eve in Eden. But Jesus "was fitted for the conflict by the indwelling of the Holy Spirit."[4] The prophet Isaiah speaks of this divine companion with Jesus by saying, "Behold my servant, whom I uphold, my chosen, in whom my soul delights; I have put my spirit upon him. . . . He will not fail or be discouraged" (Isa. 42:1-4). Jesus Himself quoted this Isaiahnic promise about the Spirit and applied it to Himself in His contention with the Pharisees after the healing of a lame man on the Sabbath (see Matt. 12:10-21).

During His temptation in the wilderness the Spirit reminded Jesus of Deuteronomy 8:3; 6:16; and 6:13, which He had previously studied and learned. With these—the sword of the Spirit—He met and quashed the temptations. By His use of this mighty weapon He routed the enemy. Three times the tempter ventured forward in subtle attack, and once he himself tried to use the sword of the Spirit to overpower Jesus. But Satan misused the Word by quoting only part of God's promise, when he challenged Jesus to fling Himself down from the pinnacle of the temple.

This is Satan's customary use of God's Word. When accosting Eve in Eden he also used only part of it by promising Eve that she would be like God by having her eyes opened. That time he won a victory with a partial truth.

The temptation in the wilderness was a climactic meeting between Jesus and Satan. Jesus had met him before; he would meet him many times and under different circumstances in the future. He even met him in the words of His close friend and disciple when Peter advised Jesus not to submit to death. But Jesus recognized Satan even when he spoke through a friend and "turned and said to Peter, 'Get behind me, Satan! You are a hindrance to me; for you are not on the side of God, but of men" (Matt. 16:23). At this time "Satan was trying to discourage Jesus, and turn Him from His mission; and Peter, in his blind love, was giving voice to the temptation. The prince of evil was the author of the thought. His instigation was behind that impressive appeal."[5]

At the trial preceding the crucifixion Satan egged the mob on in cruelty to Jesus. He "hoped that such mockery and violence would call forth from the Son of God some complaint or murmur; or that He would manifest His divine power and wrench Himself from the grasp of the multitude, and that thus the plan of salvation might at last fail."[6]

"Christ was put to the closest test, requiring the strength of all His faculties to resist the inclination when in danger, to use His power to deliver

Himself from peril, and triumph over the power of the prince of darkness. Satan showed his knowledge of the weak points of the human heart, and put forth his utmost power to take advantage of the weakness of the humanity which Christ had assumed."[7]

In the Garden of Gethsemane Jesus agonized with His Father to take the bitter cup of death away from Him, if possible. But as it was His Father's will that Jesus give His life for lost man, Jesus did not insist on His own preference, but He accepted His Father's plan for Him and drank the bitter cup of death on Calvary. He had come to save man. And since there was no way of saving both us and Himself from death, He chose to save us in accordance with the covenant He had made with the Father before the world began (see 2 Tim. 1:9, KJV).

Jesus was raised from the dead through the Spirit. Peter says that He was "made alive in the spirit" (1 Peter 3:18; compare Rom. 8:11). The Spirit was part of the resurrection power, but as the Trinity is one in purpose, motive, and acts, the other two members of the Godhead also participated in the resurrection. In Ephesians 1:17-20 Paul says that the Father raised Jesus from the dead. Before His crucifixion Jesus averred that He not merely was going to lay down His life but that He also had power to take it back (see John 10:17, 18). Jesus is rather than was—the resurrection and the life" (John 11:25). As such He had power to break the bonds of death.

Through the incarnation God became man in Jesus. To the human mind the incarnation is a mystery, hidden in the divinity. We cannot explain it; we just accept it.

The apostle Paul says that God sent "his own Son in the likeness of sinful flesh" (Rom. 8:3), "being born in the likeness of men" (Phil. 2:7), and that "he had to be made like his brethren in every respect" (Heb. 2:17). For this reason "he took not on him the nature of angels; but he took on him the seed of Abraham" (Heb. 2:16, KJV).

The apostle takes pain to show that Jesus was verily a true man, for only as such could He do His high-priestly work.

"Christ did not make believe take human nature; He did verily take it. He did in reality possess human nature."[8] "Christ bore the sins and infirmities of the race as they existed when He came to the earth to help man. In behalf of the race, with the weaknesses of fallen man upon Him, He was to stand the temptations of Satan upon all points wherewith man would be assailed."[9] "Like every child of Adam He accepted the results of the working of the great law of God."[10]

Jesus bore a physical body, formed after the human body which is affected by sin. Still, He had no connection with sin, since the sin which clung to the human body He assumed did not affect His character and had no power over Him. Jesus took the likeness in form and appearance of man, but there was a definite distinction in essence.[11]

But even though our Savior assumed and lived among men "in the likeness of sinful flesh" (Rom. 8:3), "we should have no misgivings in regard to the perfect sinlessness of the human nature of Christ."[12] Jesus did not stain with sin even the weak human nature He assumed. "In His human nature He maintained the purity of His divine character."[13] "He was perfect, and undefiled by sin."[14]

Hebrews 2:17 says that "he had to be made like his brethren in every respect" (or as in the KJV "it behooved him to be made like unto his brethren"). The word from which *had to* or *behooved* is translated is "'used of necessity imposed either by law and duty, or by reason, or by the times, or by the nature of the matter under consideration' (Thayer). Here it was the nature of the case which imposed the obligation."[15]

If God had given Jesus a different human nature from what we possess—apart from experimental acquaintance with sin—He could not be our Savior. Further, Satan would instantly have charged Him and His Father with a fake—that He was not a real man, and that even if He, possessing a nature different from ours, was able to live above sin, man could not and should not be expected to do so.

"We need not place the obedience of Christ by itself, as something for which He was particularly adapted, by His particular divine nature. . . . If Christ had a special power which it is not the privilege of man to have, Satan would have made capital of this matter. The work of Christ was to take from the claims of Satan his control of man, and He could do this only in the way that He came—a man, tempted as a man, rendering the obedience of a man."[16]

Paul is affirming that when Christ came into the world, He stood under the same conditions as we. In some way, Paul is convinced, Jesus stood under the power of sin, although sin found no response and no place in Christ. Out of "the flesh" arose the same temptations as for us. His body craved food when Satan offered it to Him. And the thought occurred to Him that He could obtain it by turning the stones into bread. But as soon as this thought registered in His conscious awareness, He resolutely repulsed it, even as He rejected the subtle temptation that came to Him through Peter, when he suggested that Jesus should not permit Himself to be killed at Jerusalem. To that temptation Jesus had instantly replied, "Get thee behind me, Satan!" (Matt. 16:23).

In this, and in all temptations, Jesus was the master over temptation and sin. Christ overcame sin in its own realm, when He Himself assumed the form of sinful flesh. "Throughout the ages the Church has confessed that Christ took upon Himself real human nature from the virgin Mary, not as it was before the fall, but such as it had become *by* and *after* the fall.

"This is clearly stated in Heb. ii. 14, 15. . . . Upon the authority of the divine Word we cannot doubt then that the Son of God became man in our fallen nature."[17]

With a body framed in the likeness of sinful flesh, the intrinsically sinless Christ became the representative of sinful mankind. It was to be right in sin's own realm that the Son was to bring sin to judgment, overcome it, and take away its power.[18]

"If He did not have man's nature, He could not be our example. If He was not a partaker of our nature, He could not have been tempted as man has been. If it were not possible for Him to yield to temptation, He could not be our helper."[19] "Had He not been fully human, Christ could not have been our substitute."[20]

"When we give to His human nature a power that it is not possible for man to have in his conflicts with Satan, we destroy the completeness of His humanity."[21]

During the incarnation Christ did not, however, part with His divinity. But "laying aside His royal robe and kingly crown, Christ clothed His divinity with humanity . . . He veiled His divinity with the garb of humanity, but He did not part with His divinity."[22] "In Christ, divinity and humanity were combined."[23]

Being both God and man, Jesus possessed both a divine and a human nature. "He [Paul] presents before us His [Christ's] two natures, divine and human."[24] "The two natures were mysteriously blended in one person-the man Christ Jesus."[25]

Only persons can sin. Objects such as trees and stones do not sin. Nor do animals sin. Nor do natures sin. Only persons endowed with minds, intelligence, and capability of making choices can sin. Jesus possessed two natures: a divine nature and a human nature. These two natures through the incarnation were blended in one person Jesus Christ. He defiled neither of His two natures with sin. Jesus was sinless.

In His human nature Jesus conquered Satan. "The enemy was overcome by Christ in His human nature. The power of the Savior's Godhead was hidden. He overcame in human nature, relying upon God for power."[26] But "Christ in His humanity was dependent upon divine power. 'I can of Mine own self do nothing,' He declared. John 5:30."[27]

It was divine power, aiding His human nature, that enabled Jesus to meet every trial and temptation victoriously. In His own strength, as a mere man, He could never have been victorious.

"Christ's humanity alone could never have endured this test [the temptation on appetite in the wilderness], but His divine power combined with humanity gained in behalf of man an infinite victory."[28] "All that was possible for man to endure in the conflict with Satan, Christ endured in His human and divine nature combined. Obedient, sinless to the last, He died for man, his substitute and surety, enduring all that men ever endure from the deceiving tempter, that man may overcome by being a partaker of the divine nature."[29]

But if Jesus during His incarnation possessed a "fallen," "sinful" nature as we do, why did not Jesus succumb to temptation and sin as every human being has done? Ultimately, "it is a mystery that is left unexplained to mortals that Christ could be tempted in all points like as we are, and yet be without sin. The incarnation of Christ has ever been, and will ever remain, a mystery."[30] But these thoughts may help us understand: "He took upon Himself fallen, suffering human nature, degraded and defiled by sin."[31] "In taking upon Himself man's nature in its fallen condition, Christ did not in the least participate in its sin."[32] "He took upon His sinless nature our sinful nature, that He might know how to succor those that are tempted."[33]

Humanly speaking, the secret lies in our different relationships to the Spirit and the divine power available to man through Him. Jesus chose at all times and under all circumstances to ally Himself with His Father and thereby experienced the indwelling of the Father through the ministry of the Holy Spirit. During His sojourn on earth Jesus did nothing on His own. He remained constantly alert to His Father's will through the Holy Spirit. In John 8:29 Jesus says about His relationship to His Father: "I always do what is pleasing to him." He subordinated His will to His Father's will.

Throughout His entire ministry Jesus chose to be led moment by moment and day by day by the Spirit. He unreservedly committed Himself to the doing of His Father's will, as unveiled to Him in the sacred scrolls and the promptings of the Spirit. His submission to His Father's will in Gethsemane illustrates this attitude. He did not insist on preserving His physical life; He chose to die rather than go against His Father's will. "For our sake He exercised a self-control stronger than hunger or death."[34] He crucified His own inclinations, although He had no more desire to die than do you and I. He pleaded with His Father to take that cup of suffering away, if possible. But He would rather die at 33 than go contrary to His Father's will by preserving His life.

Jesus could easily have escaped death. He would only have had to perform a few miracles before King Herod, and the king would instantly have released Him.[35] But He had not come to this earth to play safe or to save Himself; He came to save man—you and me—drowned and dead in sin (see Eph. 2:1). This was His constant purpose as He was directed and sustained by the Spirit.

Being filled with the Spirit, "not for one moment was there in Him an evil propensity"[36] or a favorable disposition or yearning for sin. The Spirit and sin cannot dwell in the same mind at the same time, for "if His Spirit abides in the heart, sin cannot dwell there."[37]

Jesus had no propensity for sin, and we are not to "set Him before the people as a man with the propensities of sin."[38] This becomes self-evident when we notice how Ellen White defines propensity: "Self-indulgence, self-pleasing, pride, and extravagance must be renounced. We cannot be Christians and gratify these propensities."[39] According to this definition propensities are cherished desires. In the mind and thought of Jesus there was not for a moment a favorable disposition or bias toward sin or variance from His Father's will. He set His mind as a flint to do His Father's will (see Isa. 50:7).

Righteousness consists not merely in right doing and speaking, but also in right thinking and feeling; and "the thoughts and feelings combined make up the moral character."[40] When, therefore, evil suggestions came to Jesus through the tempter to turn the stones into bread, to jump down from the pinnacle of the temple and to bow down to worship him in order to regain the world in an easier way than by going over Calvary's hill, He instantly repulsed them. These ideas never found lodgment in His mind. As soon as the possibility registered in His conscious awareness, Jesus instantly rejected the idea. "Never, in any way, leave the slightest impression upon human minds that a taint of, or inclination to, corruption rested upon Christ, or that He in any way yielded to corruption."[41]

You and I have at times chosen to sin in thought, although we have refrained from engaging in the sinful act. But even though we did not sin in deed, by admitting the thought into our thinking, we yielded to temptation and verily sinned. In the Sermon on the Mount, Jesus identified sinful thoughts as sin by saying that "every one who is angry with his brother shall be liable to judgment"; and "every one who looks at a woman lustfully has already committed adultery with her in his heart" (Matt. 5:22, 28).

"Christ did not possess the same sinful, corrupt, fallen disloyalty we possess."[42] If an unmarried woman accepts a date with an eligible man, she does so without being condemned by anyone. But if a married woman does the same, or even considers it, she is disloyal to her husband. Jesus was never disloyal to His Father. He did not entertain Satan's propositions. You and I, alas, have often done so by considering his temptations. Jesus chose not to do this. "Not even by a thought did He yield to temptation."[43]

"Let every human being be warned from the ground of making Christ altogether human, such an one as ourselves; for it cannot be."[44] Indeed, He was not like us, who often accept Satan's overtures favorably, and entertain and consider them, and in this way are disloyal to God, who has espoused us as His bride.

Without our thinking about or contemplating the possibility of a certain sinful act, the desire or passion or intense feeling for it never develops. Some of us at some time or another may have thought of some sin until it developed into an uncontrollable passion.

Thus, about passions in relation to Jesus, Ellen White says, "He is a brother in our infirmities, but not in possessing like passions."[45]

"He was a mighty petitioner, not possessing the passions of our human, fallen natures, but compassed with like infirmities, tempted in all points even as we are."[46] He did have the human nature or capacity of being acted on by external agents or forces, but He chose not to be swayed by them from His loyalty to His Father. About this Ellen White says, "Though He had all the strength of passion of humanity, never did He yield to temptation to do one single act which was not pure and elevating and ennobling."[47]

Jesus was always willingly obedient to the divine voice that spoke to Him. He subordinated His human nature to His divine nature and His human will to His divine will. "In Christ there was a *subjection of the human to the divine*. He clothed His divinity with humanity, and *placed His own person under obedience to divinity.* . . . In His humanity, Christ was obedient to all His Father's commandments."[48] You and I usually know God's will, but at times we have insisted on having our way rather than going God's way. This Jesus never did. May God forgive us for our willfulness.

Through His constant submission to the guidance of the Spirit Jesus met the full requirement of His Father's law. His soul and character were and remained pure; and only thoughts prompted by the Spirit, and thus pleasing to His Father, filled His mind. "He united humanity with divinity: a divine spirit dwelt in a temple of flesh."[49]

[1] Ellen G. White, *Education,* pp. 80, 81.

[2] Ellen G. White, *The Desire of Ages,* p. 70.

[3] Ellen G. White, *Testimonies,* vol. 1, p. 482.

[4] Ellen G. White, *The Desire of Ages,* p. 123.

[5] *Ibid.,* p. 416.

[6] Ellen G. White, *The Story of Redemption* (Washington, D.C.: Review and Herald Pub. Assn., 1947), p. 213.

[7] Ellen G. White Comments, *Seventh-day Adventist Bible Commentary,* vol. 7, p. 930.

[8] Ellen G. White, *Selected Messages,* bk. 1, p. 247.

[9] *Ibid.,* pp. 267, 268.

[10] Ellen G. White, *The Desire of Ages,* p. 49.

[11] See Gerhard Friedrich, ed., *Theological Dictionary of the Old Testament* (Grand Rapids, Mich.: William B. Eerdmans Publishing House, 1970), vol. 5, pp. 195, 196.

[12] Ellen G. White Comments, *Seventh-day Adventist Bible Commentary,* vol. 5, p. 1131.

[13] Ellen G. White, *My Life Today,* p. 323.

[14] Ellen G. White, *The Spirit of Prophecy* (Battle Creek, Mich.: Seventh-day Adventist Pub. Assn., 1877), vol. 2, p. 11.

[15] *The Expositor's Greek Testament* (Grand Rapids, Mich.: William B. Eerdmans Publishing House, n.d.), vol. 4, p. 269.

[16] Ellen G. White Comments, *Seventh-day Adventist Bible Commentary,* vol. 7, p. 930.

[17] Abraham Kuyper, *The Work of the Holy Spirit* (Grand Rapids, Mich.: William B. Eerdmans Publishing House, 1975), p. 84.

[18] Anders Nygren, *Commentary on Romans* (Philadelphia: Muhlenberg Press, 1949), pp. 313 315.

[19] Ellen G. White Comments, *Seventh-day Adventist Bible Commentary,* vol. 5, p. 1082.

[20] Ellen G. White, *Signs of the Times,* June 17, 1897.

[21] Ellen G. White Comments, *Seventh-day Adventist Bible Commentary,* vol. 7, p. 929.

[22] Ellen G. White, *Review and Herald,* June 15, 1905.

[23] Ellen G. White, *Selected Messages,* bk. 1, p. 408.

[24] Ellen G. White Comments, *Seventh-day Adventist Bible Commentary,* vol. 5, p. 1126.

[25] *Ibid.*

[26] *Ibid.,* p. 1108.

[27] Ellen G. White, *The Desire of Ages,* pp. 674, 675.

[28] Ellen G. White, *Confrontation* (Washington, D.C.: Review and Herald Pub. Assn., 1971), pp. 66, 67.

[29] Ellen G. White, *Selected Messages,* bk. 1, p. 342.

[30] Ellen G. White Comments, *Seventh-day Adventist Bible Commentary,* vol. 5, pp. 1128, 1129.

[31] Ellen G. White Comments, *Seventh-day Adventist Bible Commentary,* vol. 4, p. 1147.

[32] *Ibid.,* vol. 5, p. 1131.

[33] Ellen G. White, *Medical Ministry* (Mountain View, Calif.: Pacific Press Pub. Assn., 1932), p. 181.

[34] Ellen G. White, *The Desire of Ages,* p. 117.

[35] *Ibid.,* pp. 729-731.

[36] Ellen G. White Comments, *Seventh-day Adventist Bible Commentary,* vol. 5, p. 1128.

[37] Ellen G. White, *Review and Herald,* Mar. 16, 1886.

[38] Ellen G. White Comments, *Seventh-day Adventist Bible Commentary,* vol. 5, p. 1128.

[39] Ellen G. White, *Review and Herald,* May 16, 1893.

[40] Ellen G. White, *Testimonies,* vol. 5, p. 310.

[41] Ellen G. White Comments, *Seventh-day Adventist Bible Commentary,* vol. 5, p. 1128.

[42] Ellen G. White, manuscript 94, 1893.

[43] Ellen G. White, *The Desire of Ages,* p. 123.

[44] Ellen G. White Comments, *Seventh-day Adventist Bible Commentary,* vol. 5, p. 1129.

[45] Ellen G. White, *Testimonies,* vol. 2, pp. 201, 202.

[46] *Ibid.,* p. 509.

[47] Ellen G. White, *In Heavenly Places* (Washington, D.C.: Review and Herald Pub. Assn., 1967), p. 155.

[48] Ellen G. White, *Review and Herald,* Nov. 9, 1897.

[49] Ellen G. White Comments, *Seventh-day Adventist Bible Commentary,* vol. 4, p. 1147.

CHAPTER 4

The Promise of the Spirit

Already in Old Testament times the Spirit was spoken of as a present reality among the followers of God. Isaiah reminds us that God had placed His Spirit among the Israelites in the days of Moses by saying, "But they rebelled and grieved his holy Spirit. . . . Where is he who put in the midst of them his holy Spirit?" (Isa. 63:10, 11). Eldad and Medad, among the Israelites, received the Spirit (see Num. 11:26). Moses on that occasion expressed the wish that all the people might be recipients of the Spirit, as he himself was. Othniel, Caleb's younger brother, received the Spirit after the Israelites had settled in Canaan (see Judges 3:9, 10).

David's penitential prayer after his great sin indicates that he had been the object of the Spirit's work. "Cast me not away from thy presence, and take not thy holy Spirit from me" (Ps. 51:11). He also exclaims: "Whither shall I go from thy Spirit?" (Ps. 139:7).

Micah exclaims, "I am filled with power, with the Spirit of the Lord" (Micah 3:8). Ezekiel writes: "The Spirit of the Lord fell upon me, and he said to me, 'Say, Thus says the Lord: So you think, O house of Israel; for I know the things that come into your mind" (Eze. 11:5). Haggai assures His people that the Spirit is with them. "I am with you, says the Lord of hosts. . . . My Spirit abides among you; fear not" (Hag. 2:4, 5).

Of John the Baptist the angel said: "He will be great before the Lord, and he shall drink no wine nor strong drink, and he will be filled with the Holy Spirit, even from his mother's womb" (Luke 1:15).

The Spirit is omnipresent; He is everywhere. But it does not follow that He lives and dwells in or with every living, intelligent, free-willed being. Satan and his fallen angels are also intelligent, free-willed beings, but the Spirit is not with them, although it was God's original design that He should guide both angels and men.

The Spirit acts upon a human being in two ways, either from without or from within. He comes to the unconverted and speaks to him from without. Jesus came to Saul in that way on the Damascus road, and the Spirit does the same. But to be a saving and transforming influence He must dwell within a person and work from within. This can happen only with the person's consent and choice.

Many Old Testament writers promise that the Spirit will be poured out in the future. Through Solomon, under the symbol of wisdom, Jesus promises, "Behold, I will pour, out my spirit unto you, I will make known my words unto you" (Prov. 1:23, KJV). Isaiah looks forward to the time when the Spirit will be poured out upon the world and make the spiritually barren blossom as the rose: "Until the Spirit be poured upon us from on high, and the wilderness becomes a fruitful field, and the fruitful field is deemed a forest" (Isa. 32:15).

Ezekiel, in addition to speaking of Him as a present reality in his own life, presents the most beautiful promise of the Spirit's outpouring in the future: "Then will I sprinkle clean water upon you, and ye shall be clean: from all your filthiness, and from all your idols, will I cleanse you. A new heart also will I give you, and a new spirit will I put within you: and I will take away the stony heart out of your flesh, and I will give you an heart of flesh. And I will put my spirit within you, and cause you to walk in my statutes, and ye shall keep my judgments, and do them" (Eze. 36:25-27, KJV). The prophet Joel designates the last days for the copious outpouring of the Spirit (see Joel 2:28, 29).

Although John the Baptist was filled with the Spirit from his birth (see Luke 1:15), in his preaching he pointed to the Messiah, who was to baptize His followers with the Spirit: "I baptize you with water for repentance, but he who is coming after me is mightier than I, whose sandals I am not worthy to carry; he will baptize you with the Holy Spirit and with fire" (Matt. 3:11). His own water baptism was but a symbol of the Spirit's cleansing from sin; it would not fit his hearers to stand in the presence of a Holy God.

To the listening multitudes at the Feast of Dedication Jesus said: 'If any one thirst, let him come to me, and drink. He who believes in me, as the scripture has said, "Out of his heart shall flow rivers of living water."' Now this he said about the Spirit, which those who believed in him were to receive; for as yet the Spirit had not been given, because Jesus was not yet glorified" (John 7:37-39). When Jesus spoke these words, the Spirit as a dove had already descended upon Him, and the Spirit had ministered to men and women in Old Testament times.

Nevertheless, the Spirit had not been given to men in His fullness prior to Pentecost. Gethsemane and Calvary must precede the bestowal of this gift in His fullness. It was only after Jesus had conquered death through His resurrection and "ascended up on high," leading a host of captives, released from Satan's prison house of death (see Isa. 14:17, 18), that He could give these "gifts unto men" in plenitude (Eph. 4:8, KJV).

Thus Jesus told His disciples: "I will pray the Father, and he will give you another Counselor, to be with you for ever, even the Spirit of truth" (John 14:16, 17). This is the first direct promise made by Jesus to His disciples about the Spirit. Evidently Jesus was referring to the Spirit's coming in fullness on the Day of Pentecost, even as He was referring to the same event in His renewed promise of the Spirit just before He left them (see Acts 1:4, 5). From this statement it may appear that the Pentecostal outpouring was the Spirit's first appearance on this earth. But this was obviously not so in light of the Old Testament witness. "Before this the Spirit had been in the world; from the very beginning of the work of redemption He had been moving upon men's hearts."[1] At the very time Jesus gave these promises the Spirit even dwelt in the hearts of the disciples according to Christ's words in John 14:17.

Indeed the Spirit had been on earth since Creation and "during the patriarchal age the influence of the Holy Spirit had often been revealed in a marked manner, but never in its fullness."[2] Jesus, in John 15:26, says that the Spirit proceeds from the Father. From this stems the term "procession," used in theological literature. It refers to the being, eternity, and the relation of the Spirit to the Father, in contradistinction to the term "generation" which is used to describe the relation of the Son to the Father. The present indicative tense in Greek, *proceeds,* denotes the eternal and continuous relation of the Spirit to the Father. In John 16:7 Jesus says: "I will send him to you." The Spirit is subordinate to the Father and the Son. The Father sends both the Son and the Spirit, and the Son sends the Spirit, while the Spirit sends neither the Father nor the Son.

The Nicene Creed reads: "And [I believe] in the Holy Ghost, the Lord and Giver of Life, who proceedeth from the Father [and the Son]; who with the Father and the Son together is worshiped and glorified." "And the Son"—*Filioque*—was added to the Creed at the Council of Toledo in A.D. 589. This was an interpolation of the original creed and regarded as such by the Eastern Church. As such it was one of the sore bones of contention between the Roman and Greek Churches and heavily contributed to the Great Schism in 1054.[3]

The procession of the Spirit is inscrutable, but the creed is an attempt to express in human words the relationship between the persons in the Trinity based on scriptural revelation.

Did the Spirit proceed from the Son as well as from the Father? This was a problem debated in the Western church, not in the Eastern, just as the problem of the deity of Christ was an Eastern, not a Western problem. In order to safeguard and support the belief in the deity of the Spirit, it was essential for the Eastern church to represent Him as proceeding solely from the Father. The Western church, on the other hand, started with the unity and equality of the Father and the Son and wanted to buttress this belief by stating that the Spirit proceeded from both the Father and the Son.[4]

"I will pray the Father, and he will give you another Counselor, to be with you for ever" (John 14:16). In this, as in other texts, the Spirit is called "another Counselor" ("Comforter" in KJV). This "Counselor" was coming to take the place of Jesus as the disciples' "Helper" after Christ's ascension. Undoubtedly, "Comforter" used in the King James Version is an infelicitous translation of the Greek *paraklētos*. John Wycliffe is responsible for the word "Comforter" in the English Bible, since he introduced it in his translation back in the fourteenth century.

The word "Comforter" had a different meaning in the fourteenth century from its meaning today. Then its root meaning was strength, as is that of the Latin word from which it is derived. This was also Wycliffe's meaning, for he translates Philippians 4:13: "I can do all things through Christ who comforts me." *Paraklētos* actually means one called to stand alongside another. The Spirit is a helper always at my side with His counsel, His strength and any other form of help that is needed.

The Greek word *paraklētos*, translated Comforter, means that, but much more. It is a compound word made up of *"para"* which means "alongside," and *"klētos"* which means "one called." Thus the whole word means "one called to stand alongside another," or one called to take his part to help him in every emergency that arises. The same word *paraklētos* is translated "advocate" in First John 2:1. The *New English Bible* translates it "Advocate" also in John 14:16 rather than "Comforter"; while the Revised Standard Version renders it "Counselor." "Advocate" and "Counselor" convey its meaning more accurately than does "Comforter." But it means even more than "advocate" or "counselor"; it expresses the thought of a "helper" always at hand with his counsel and his strength or any form of help needed in any conceivable emergency. Such a "Helper" is the Spirit to God's children.

Jesus was continuously to be with the disciples and all His followers. "All who keep his commandments abide in him, and he in them. And by this we know that he abides in us, by the Spirit which he has given us" (John 3:24). "By this we know that we abide in him and he in us, because he has given us of his own Spirit" (1 John 4:13).

The apostles and their fellow believers were not to be left alone or without help when Jesus ascended to heaven. Before Jesus left His disciples, He said, "Lo, I am with you alway, even unto the end of the world" (Matt. 28:20, KJV). It is through His Spirit that Jesus is to be with us. "Christ is to live in His representatives by the Spirit of truth."[5] An all-adequate Helper was to be with them. "By the Spirit, He said, He would manifest Himself to them."[6]

The Holy Spirit works also through the heavenly angels. "His [God's] angels are appointed to watch over us, and if we put ourselves under their guardianship, then in every time of danger they will be at our right hand. When unconsciously we are in danger of exerting a wrong influence, the angels will be by our side, prompting us to a better course, choosing our words for us, and influencing our actions."[7]

Jesus promised His disciples before His departure that the Spirit would be a more adequate Helper to them than even He Himself. "Nevertheless I tell you the truth: it is to your advantage that I go away, for if I do not go away, the Counselor will not come to you; but if I go, I will send him to you" (John 16:7).

Christ's imminent departure would enrich the disciples, as well as the Christians throughout the ages, rather than impoverish them. While on earth Jesus was geographically limited to one particular place. While He was with His three disciples on the top of the Mount of Transfiguration, He could not be with the other nine, helping them in their moment of need and distress. But the Paraclete, given in place of His physical presence, being omnipresent, is not cumbered by the limitations of the human body. He is equally accessible to all everywhere, irrespective of location. Jesus had been and would be, if He had remained on earth, only an external geographically limited presence; the Spirit's presence, on the other hand, would be omnipresent and internal. Hence, He would be able to do more for His followers through the Spirit than He Himself could do on earth.

"The Holy Spirit is Christ's representative, but divested of the personality of humanity, and independent thereof. Cumbered with humanity, Christ could not be in every place personally. Therefore it was for their [the disciples'] interest that He should go to the Father, and send the Spirit to be His successor on earth. No one could then have any advantage because of his location or his personal contact with Christ. By the Spirit the Savior would be accessible to all. In this sense He would be nearer to them than if He had not ascended on high."[8]

The Spirit's presence has been assured to every believer, irrespective of where he is. He desires to be the Christian's constant helper. The prophet Isaiah assures us: "When the enemy shall come in like a flood, the Spirit of the Lord shall lift up a standard against him" (Isa. 59:19, KJV). The divine commentary on this promise is this: "The enemy cannot overcome the humble learner of Christ, the one who walks prayerfully before the Lord. Christ interposes Himself as a shelter, a retreat, from the assaults of the wicked one."[9]

On the last walk Jesus took with His eleven remaining disciples, from Jerusalem out to the Mount of Olivet, He repeated His promise of the Spirit (see Acts 1:4-9). This was the last promise before He began to ascend toward heaven before their very eyes. As they returned to Jerusalem, they were intent on the fulfillment of this promise as His words lingered in their minds: "You shall receive power when the Holy Spirit has come upon you; and you shall be my witnesses in Jerusalem and in all Judea and Samaria and to the end of the earth" (Acts 1:8).

---

[1] Ellen G. White, *The Desire of Ages*, p. 669.

[2] Ellen G. White, *The Acts of the Apostles* (Mountain View, Calif.: Pacific Press Pub. Assn., 1911), p. 37.

[3] See Philip Schaff, *The Creeds of Christendom* (Grand Rapids, Mich.: Baker Book House), vol. 1, p. 26; vol. 2, p. 59; John F. Walvoord, *The Holy Spirit* (Grand Rapids, Mich.: Zondervan Publishing House, 1974), pp. 13-16.

[4] W. H. Griffith Thomas, *The Holy Spirit of God* (Grand Rapids, Mich.: William B. Eerdmans Publishing House, 1972), p. 91.

[5] Ellen G. White, *Review and Herald,* Apr. 4, 1893.

[6] Ellen G. White, *The Desire of Ages,* p. 670.

[7] Ellen G. White, *Christ's Object Lessons*, pp. 341, 342.

[8] Ellen G. White, *The Desire of Ages,* p. 669.

[9] Ellen G. White, *My Life Today,* p. 316.

CHAPTER 5

Historical Pentecost

Suddenly a sound came from heaven like the rush of a mighty wind, and it filled all the house where they were sitting. And there appeared to them tongues as of fire, distributed and resting on each one of them. And they were all filled with the Holy Spirit" (Acts 2:2-4).

Pentecost did not denote the beginning of the existence of the Spirit, or even of His ministry among men. Rather, it marked "the installation of the Holy Spirit as the Administrator of the Church in all things."[1] Upon His return to heaven Jesus committed the supervision and direction of His church to the Spirit. The Spirit is His vicegerent on earth until Jesus returns to receive His own people unto Himself.

Pentecost followed the reinstatement of Jesus at the right hand of God in heaven. It signalized His restoration to the position He had occupied with the Father before His incarnation and His installation as our High Priest in heaven. As a result, and as a sign of this, His followers received the fullness of the Spirit with His accompanying power (see Acts 2:33). "Now heaven rejoiced in being able to pour upon the church the riches of the Spirit's power."[2]

It was in this sense that John could say about the Spirit at the Feast of Unleavened Bread six months prior to the crucifixion that "as yet the Spirit had not been given" (John 7:39). At Pentecost the Holy Spirit did come in His fullness to be the official representative and successor of Jesus Christ on earth. The Spirit had not functioned before as Christ's vicegerent.

During His appearances to them after His resurrection, Jesus "charged them not to depart from Jerusalem, but to wait for the promise of the Father, which, he said, 'you heard of me, for John baptized with water, but before many days you shall be baptized with the Holy Spirit'" (Acts 1:4, 5).

The promise of the Father referred to the gift of the Spirit which Jesus had given to His disciples in John 14:16-26 and 16:7-13. The disciples were to remain or stay, or even sit (Greek: *kathisate,* Luke 24:49) in Jerusalem, until the promise was fulfilled.

To "wait" or "sit" is primarily an unstrenuous and nonsubjective condition. The emphasis is not primarily upon the activity of the disciples, but rather upon the fulfillment of God's promise. The word translated promise *(epaggelia),* in other parts of the New Testament stresses God's grace rather than man's effort. The Spirit is God's free gift in response to the believer's faith, trust, or commitment to Him and His will. It is "the *gift* of the Holy Spirit" (Acts 2:38; compare Acts 8:20; 10:45).

Jesus promised the disciples power as an accompaniment of the Spirit. "You shall receive power when the Holy Spirit has come upon you; and you shall be my witnesses in Jerusalem and in all Judea and Samaria and to the end of the earth" (Acts 1:8). In waiting for the fulfillment of the promise of the Spirit, the disciples "all continued with one accord in prayer and supplication, with the women, and Mary the mother of Jesus, and with his brethren" (Acts 1:14, KJV).

"In obedience to Christ's command, they waited in Jerusalem for the promise of the Father—the outpouring of the Spirit. They did not wait in idleness. The record says that they were 'continually in the temple, praising and blessing God.' Luke 24:53. They also met together to present their requests to the Father in the name of Jesus. They knew that they had a Representative in heaven, an Advocate at the throne of God. In solemn awe they bowed in prayer, repeating the assurance, 'Whatsoever ye shall ask the Father in My name, He will give it you. Hitherto have ye asked nothing in My name: ask, and ye shall receive, that your joy may be full.' John 16:23, 24. Higher and still higher they extended the hand of faith, with the mighty argument, 'It is Christ that died, yea rather, that is risen again, who is even at the right hand of God, who also maketh intercession for us.' Romans 8:34.

"As the disciples waited for the fulfillment of the promise, they humbled their hearts in true repentance and confessed their unbelief."[3]

During this period of waiting, the disciples became changed into new and different men. Even as late as at the Lord's Supper, Jesus had said to Peter, "when thou art converted, strengthen thy brethren" (Luke 22:32, KJV). Those among the 11 disciples who were not previously converted were genuinely converted between the time of the Lord's Supper and Pentecost. And those who were converted gained a deeper experience. While Jesus was still with them, "even the disciples, though outwardly they had left all for Jesus' sake, had not in heart ceased to seek things for themselves. It was this spirit that prompted the strife as to who should be greatest. It was this that came between them and Christ, making them so little in sympathy with His mission of self-sacrifice, so slow to comprehend the mystery of redemption."[4]

By the time of Pentecost all the disciples were living in full harmony with their understanding of God's will, and consequently in complete harmony one with another. They were all of one accord and thus ready to be filled with the Spirit.

"It was after the disciples had come into perfect unity, when they were no longer striving for the highest place, that the Spirit was poured out. They were of one accord. All differences had been put away. And the testimony borne of them after the Spirit had been given is the same. Mark the word: 'The multitude of them that believed were of one heart and of one soul.' The Spirit of Him who died that sinners might live, animated the entire congregation of believers."[5]

But the outpouring of the Spirit was not solely dependent on the spiritual experience of the disciples and their fellow believers. Their spiritual readiness had to be matched by Christ's reinstatement in His preincarnatjon position in heaven.

"Christ's ascension to heaven was the signal that His followers were to receive the promised blessing. For this they were to wait before they entered upon their work. When Christ passed within the heavenly gates, He was enthroned amidst the adoration of the angels. As soon as this ceremony was completed, the Holy Spirit descended upon the disciples in rich currents, and Christ was indeed glorified, even with the glory which He had with the Father from all eternity. The Pentecostal outpouring was Heaven's communication that the Redeemer's inauguration was accomplished. According to His promise He had sent the Holy Spirit from heaven to His followers as a token that He had, as priest and king, received all authority in heaven and on earth, and was the Anointed One over His people."[6]

With the reception of the fullness of the Spirit at Pentecost, it became crystal clear to the disciples that they had a friend and intercessor at the throne of God in heaven. And when any truth becomes central and vital, there comes a desire to communicate that truth. The disciples wanted others to learn about what God had done through Christ. It led them to witness for God. But to do this, the Spirit-filled believers needed a knowledge of other languages. In answer to their yearning to tell the story of salvation to others, God bestowed the gift of tongues, or other languages, on the apostles and the believers so that they could witness effectively to those from other countries.

"They were all filled with the Holy Spirit and began to speak in other tongues, as the Spirit gave them utterance" (Acts 2:4). "The Holy Spirit, assuming the form of tongues of fire, rested upon those assembled. This was an emblem of the gift then bestowed on the disciples, which enabled them to speak with fluency languages with which they had heretofore been unacquainted. The appearance of fire signified the fervent zeal with which the apostles would labor and the power that would attend their work."[7]

Every known language was represented by the crowds gathered in Jerusalem for the feast of Pentecost. "This diversity of languages would have been a great hindrance to the proclamation of the gospel; God therefore in a miraculous manner supplied the deficiency of the apostles. The Holy Spirit did for them that which they could not have accomplished for themselves in a lifetime. They could now proclaim the truths of the gospel abroad, speaking with accuracy the languages of those for whom they were laboring. This miraculous gift was a strong evidence to the world that their commission bore the signet of Heaven."[8]

The apostle Peter in giving his explanation of the happenings at Pentecost quoted the prophecy of Joel and applied that prophecy to the miraculous outpouring of the Holy Spirit on that memorable day (see Acts 2:14-21).

The Spirit does not work by Himself; He works through men, and after Pentecost the believers were willing to be guided by the Spirit and do His biddings. When the Holy Spirit on the Day of Pentecost brought 3000 people to repentance, He worked through the disciples and their fellow believers. Every conversion spoken of in the book of Acts was through the agency of a believer already saved. Even the apostle Paul who met Jesus on the Damascus Road was sought out by the disciple Ananias before he was brought into God's church. And Ananias was brought on the scene through a heavenly vision (see Acts 9:10-17).

While the deacon Philip was "still in Samaria, he was directed by a heavenly messenger to 'go toward the south unto the way that goeth down from Jerusalem unto Gaza. . . . And he arose and went.' He did not question the call, nor did he hesitate to obey; for he had learned the lesson of conformity to God's will."[9]

The Spirit also led Peter to Cornelius, the Roman centurion at Caesarea who was seeking for truth. An angel appeared to Cornelius, but the angel did not tell Cornelius what to do in order to be saved. Rather, the angel told him, "Send men to Joppa, and call for Simeon, whose surname is Peter; who shall tell thee words, whereby thou and all thy house shall be saved" (Acts 11:13, 14).

Such was the experience of the believers after Pentecost. Human instrumentalities were guided by the Spirit, and heavenly visions and conversions were effected. Today, the Holy Spirit is waiting for you and me to be willing to do His biddings and be mouthpieces for Him in speaking to men who are seeking for truth. The Holy Spirit has chosen to reach the unsaved through those who have already claimed Jesus as their Lord and Savior and who already belong to His church.

The Pentecostal infilling of the Spirit was not a temporary and final infilling. When Peter and John were later called before the Sanhedrin to give an account of their activities, they were filled with the Spirit. The Scriptures say: "Then Peter, filled with the Holy Spirit, said to them, 'Rulers of the people and elders'" (Acts 4:8).

The infilling of the Spirit, experienced by the apostles at Pentecost, continued as an abiding presence of the Spirit in their lives. This made the difference between Peter's behavior now from what it had been at the time of the trial of Jesus. Peter and John stood now before some of the very men before whom Peter had shamefully denied his Lord. Peter remembered his disgraceful denial of his Lord and took the opportunity of redeeming his cowardice.

"With holy boldness and in the power of the Spirit Peter fearlessly declared: 'Be it known unto you all, and to all the people of Israel, that by the name of Jesus Christ of Nazareth, whom ye crucified, whom God raised from the dead, even by him doth this man stand here before you whole.'"[10] Being filled with the Spirit, the disciples were fearless in their witness for Jesus as the only Savior (see Acts 4:12).

The preaching of the disciples was seconded by the Spirit. "We are witnesses to these things, and so is the Holy Spirit whom God has given to those who obey him" (Acts 5:32). Through the imbuement of this divine power the disciples went out and evangelized the then known world in 30 years (see Col. 1:23).

The church, like the group of disciples, is made up of many members. But although many, and coming from different backgrounds, they move in unison, not at cross-purposes one with another. Despite the many personalities united in the church body, there will be no disharmony when they are all led by the same Spirit. The genuineness and the totality of the Spirit's leadership in a church may be judged by its unity.

[1] James Elder Cumming, D.D., cited by A. J. Gordon in *The Ministry of the Spirit* (Minneapolis: Bethany Fellowship Inc., 1964), p. 128.

[2] Ellen G. White, *Testimonies,* vol. 7, p. 31.

[3] Ellen G. White, *The Acts of the Apostles,* pp. 35, 36.

[4] Ellen G. White, *The Desire of Ages,* p. 409.

[5] Ellen G. White, *Signs of the Times,* Feb. 17, 1914.

[6] Ellen G. White, *The Acts of the Apostles,* pp. 38, 39.

[7] *Ibid.,* p. 39.

[8] *Ibid.,* pp. 39, 40.

[9] *Ibid.,* p. 107.

[10] *Ibid.,* p. 63.

CHAPTER 6

Being Baptized With and Filled With the Spirit

Seven passages in the New Testament speak about Spirit baptism. Five of these are prophetic and speak about this baptism as being in the future. Of these, four are the Evangelists' records of John the Baptist's words that Christ was to baptize with the Holy Spirit, while John had baptized in water (see Matt. 3:11; Mark 1:8; Luke 3:16; John 1:33).

Just before His ascension Jesus reiterated these words of John to His disciples, telling them that soon they were to be baptized with the Spirit (see Acts 1:5). From Peter's report to the church at Jerusalem about the events at the house of Cornelius, it is evident that the disciples understood this prophecy of John the Baptist, reiterated by Jesus, to have been fulfilled at Pentecost (see Acts 11:15, 16). This one passage speaking about Spirit baptism is historical, since it refers back to the Pentecostal outpouring of the Spirit. These six references about Spirit baptism all refer to the experience on the day of Pentecost, as originally prophesied by John the Baptist.

The seventh and last passage concerning Spirit baptism is in 1 Corinthians 12. Verse 13 reads: "By one Spirit we were all baptized into one body—Jews or Greeks, slaves or free—and all were made to drink of one Spirit." Paul is the only one apart from John the Baptist who speaks of Spirit baptism. In addition to these texts on Spirit baptism, several verses refer to the Spirit, using the terms "filled with," or "full of," "the Spirit fell on," and similar expressions.

When the prophecy of John the Baptist was fulfilled on the Day of Pentecost, Luke does not speak of it as a Spirit baptism, but he says that "they were all filled with the Holy Spirit" (Acts 2:4). Of the outpouring of the Holy Spirit on Cornelius's household Peter says that the Spirit "fell on" the hearers, but he likens the event to the outpouring of the Holy Spirit at Pentecost (see Acts 11:15, 16). Luke, in writing about this event, uses the same expression (see Acts 10:44). Nevertheless, he refers to it as a fulfillment of the words of Jesus in which he pointed back to John's prophecy (see Acts 11:15, 16; 1:4, 5).

At Pentecost the believers were both baptized with and filled with the Spirit. But because the baptism and the filling with the Spirit occurred simultaneously, they have often been looked upon as being the same experience. But this they are not. Luke reports that after Pentecost the believers were "filled with" the Spirit several times (see Acts 2:4; 4:8, 31; 9:17; 13:9, 52).

There is a difference between being baptized with the Spirit and being filled with the Spirit. Paul says that "by one Spirit we were all baptized into one body—Jews or Greeks, slaves or free—and all were made to drink of one Spirit" (1 Cor. 12:13). In his metaphor in 1 Corinthians 12 Paul likens the church, or the body of Christ, to the human body. When a sinner accepts Christ as his Savior, he becomes a member of "the body of Christ" (1 Cor. 12:27). Christ Himself is the head of the body (see Eph. 5:23), and by Spirit baptism each new member joins this body.

It is the Spirit that draws us to Christ while we are still dead in sin. As the sinner hears and responds to the pleadings of the Spirit to his heart and surrenders his life to God, "the Spirit of God through faith produces a new life in the soul."[1] "Unless one is born of water and the Spirit, he cannot enter the kingdom of God" (John 3:5). God now gives or baptizes him with the Spirit. The verbs in the Greek "were baptized" and "were made to drink" (1 Cor. 12:13) both indicate a singular—a once-for-all—action in past time.

God gives the Spirit, or baptizes the true believer with the Spirit, in response to the person's belief or trust in Him. He is thus born by the Spirit and sealed with the Spirit (see Eph. 1:13, 14). The Spirit is given him as an earnest (guarantee) of his final and full salvation, with deliverance from sin and its realm (see 2 Cor. 5:5). If a person has not received the Spirit, he is not a Christian. The apostle Paul emphatically asserts this by saying, "Any one who does not have the Spirit of Christ does not belong to him" (Rom. 3:9). Without the Spirit a person is not part of the body of Christ.

"Through the Spirit the believer becomes a partaker of the divine nature."[2] New life in conversion and Spirit baptism are to precede water baptism. Water baptism is but an outward demonstration that the old self is dead. In the baptismal waters it is symbolically buried. When the person rises from the baptismal water, he testifies that he has become "a partaker of the divine nature" through the indwelling of the Holy Spirit.

Without the Holy Spirit we are not alive in Christ. Rather, we are like

Ezekiel's valley of dry bones about which Ellen White says: "Not only does this simile of the dry bones apply to the world, but also to those who have been blessed with great light; for they also are like the skeletons of the valley. They have the form of men, the framework of the body; but they have not spiritual life. But the parable does not leave the dry bones merely knit together into the form of men; for it is not enough that there is symmetry of limb and feature. The breath of life must vivify the bodies, that they might stand upright, and spring into activity. These bones represent the house of Israel, the church of God, and the hope of the church is the vivifying influence of the Holy Spirit. The Lord must breathe upon the dry bones, that they may live."[3]

The Spirit has taken up His abode in every person who has accepted Christ as his personal Savior. It is the indwelling of the Spirit that makes him a Christian. The apostle John says: "By this we know that he [Jesus] abides in us, by the Spirit which he has given us" (1 John 3:24). His indwelling is manifested by the Spirit (see 2 Tim. 1:14). The Spirit becomes our endowment when we are adopted into God's family (see Gal. 4:6).

Peter makes it plain that we receive the Spirit upon conversion. "Peter said to them, 'Repent, and be baptized every one of you in the name of Jesus Christ for the forgiveness of your sins; and you shall receive the gift of the Holy Spirit'" (Acts 2:38).

The Spirit is a guest in our soul temple (see 1 Cor. 3:16; 6:19). But He is a guest as the pilot on a ship is a guest; He has been invited to take control, as the captain of the ship invites the pilot to take over the navigation of the ship. So the Spirit has come in to direct our choices. Consequently, no other authority shall ideally be known and recognized in our lives than that of the Holy Spirit. He is our pilot; we have surrendered the navigation of our lives to Him.

Obedience is a prerequisite for the Spirit's abiding presence with the believer. It is the Spirit that enables us to obey. Peter says we are "sanctified by the Spirit for obedience to Jesus Christ" (1 Peter 1:2). It is impossible for man himself to produce obedience apart from the Spirit's help. This sequence is also presented in Acts 5:32 which reads: "We are witnesses to these things, and so is the Holy Spirit whom God has given to those who obey him." The verb tenses, in the Greek original, lucidly show that God *gave* His Spirit to those who are continuously obeying. The gift of the Spirit precedes obedience, but God permits His Spirit, as His seal, to remain with those who continue to obey Him.

Neither does God take His Spirit away from us at our first disobedience. If He did, all of us would be eternally lost. He suffers long with us and stays with us as long as there is some hope. He is grieved when His authority is slighted. But as long as we have not conclusively decided to spurn His will, He remains, hoping that gradually He will be in full control of the soul temple.

The experience of Saul in the Old Testament may serve as an illustration of the Spirit's work with a person. When God, through Samuel, chose Saul as Israel's first king, Saul in humility responded to God's invitation to him (see 1 Sam. 9:21). He accepted God as his helper, and "God gave Saul a new nature" (1 Sam. 10:9, TEV). The Spirit came upon him (see 1 Sam. 10:6, 9, 10). After this he was filled with the Spirit at least once more (see 1 Sam. 11:6). God gave Saul the Spirit that he might be able to obey and to do His work.

When Saul was called to the throne, he was deficient in both knowledge and experience and had serious defects of character. "But the Lord granted him the Holy Spirit as a guide and helper, and placed him in a position where he could develop the qualities requisite for a ruler of Israel. Had he remained humble, seeking constantly to be guided by divine wisdom, he would have been enabled to discharge the duties of his high position with success and honor. Under the influence of divine grace every good quality would have been gaining strength, while evil tendencies would have lost their power."[4]

But even though Saul had received the Spirit, he began to follow his own notions and turn away from God in repeated and continuous disobedience. He became self-assertive and stubborn. No longer was he willing to be guided by God through His Spirit. Then "the Spirit of the Lord departed from Saul, and an evil spirit from the Lord tormented him" (1 Sam. 16:14).

God did not remove His Spirit from Saul at his first disobedience. He left His representative with him, hoping that the temporarily obstinate Saul would change his attitude.

Nations do not withdraw their ambassadors from one another at the first disagreement. They leave them to discuss issues and policies, hoping that the temporary disagreement will be ironed out. But if the contentions remain and become irreconcilable, the ambassadors will ultimately be withdrawn. So it is with God. If a person knowingly and consistently disobeys God, God will finally remove the seal of His Spirit from him. By doing so He declares that that person no longer belongs to Him.

If a person knowingly, willfully, and habitually disobeys God's will and still claims to enjoy the baptism of the Spirit, this experience must relate to a counterfeit spirit. And a counterfeit is bewilderingly like the genuine in appearance. As a matter of fact, many people are constantly duped by counterfeits of various kinds.

The endowment of the Spirit is therefore not necessarily for life. When even those who have received the Spirit turn away from God in disobedience, as did King Saul, the Spirit leaves them. The apostle's plea to us is therefore, "Do not grieve the Holy Spirit of God, in whom you were sealed for the day of redemption" (Eph. 4:30).

There are some who are "converted" and have verily joined a church but have not been joined to Christ. "Joining the church is one thing, and connecting with Christ is quite another. Not all the names registered in the church books are registered in the Lamb's book of life. Many, though apparently sincere believers, do not keep up a living connection with Christ. They have enlisted, they have entered their names on the register; but the inner work of grace is not wrought in the heart. As the result they are not happy, and they make hard work of serving God."[5] These have not received the Spirit baptism.

I myself gave my life to God as a young man. But I received or accepted nothing. During part of that first year I passed through a doleful experience. The only thing I could think of was what I had given up or relinquished to become a child of God. I had nothing to live for. I wanted to die.

Fortunately, I did not die. If I had died, I am sure I would have been eternally lost. After nearly a year in this dismal state, I woke up, as it were. In addition to giving up the world, I now accepted Jesus. Now the Spirit came into my life; I was baptized with the Spirit. Through this experience life became new to me. Now I had something to live for. Life beckoned me with limitless opportunities of service for Christ.

Unfortunately, I am not the only one who has lived in the vestibule to the new life in Christ. One Sabbath a few years ago, as I walked out of a large church, a friend confided to me, "If I did not know that we as Seventh-day Adventists have the truth, and that the Seventh-day Adventist Church is God's true church, I certainly would not keep the Sabbath. I don't like it." The man who made this confession is a respected church member in one of our largest churches here in the United States. He obviously had lingered in the vestibule to a live Christian experience much longer than I had.

My friend and I were like the man described in the parable in Matt. 12:43-45. Here Jesus graphically shows the spiritual disaster of merely driving out the devil from one's life. The vacant apartment must not merely be vacated of a bad tenant; the good Spirit must be invited in to fill our hearts and lives.

"The parable of the man from whom an evil spirit had been cast out, who did not fill the soul with the love of Christ, illustrates the necessity of not only emptying the heart, but of supplying the vacuum with a divine occupant. . . . The man in this parable refused to do the work of Satan; but the trouble with him was that after the heart was swept and garnished, he failed to invite the presence of the heavenly guests. It is not enough to make the heart empty; we must have the vacuum filled with the love of God. The soul must be furnished with the graces of the Spirit of God. We may leave off many bad habits, and yet not be truly sanctified, because we do not have a connection with God. We must unite with Christ."[6]

Jesus was both baptized and filled with the Spirit (see Luke 4:1; Acts 10:38). "Daily He received a fresh baptism of the Holy Spirit."[7] He gave the Spirit full control in His life; He was willingly ruled by the Spirit.

"To Jesus, who emptied Himself for the salvation of lost humanity, the Holy Spirit was given without measure. So it will be given to every follower of Christ when the whole heart is surrendered for His indwelling."[8]

After we have been baptized with the Spirit, upon our acceptance of Jesus as our Savior from sin, God hopes that we shall continue on to be filled with the Spirit and give Him full control in our lives, as the captain of a ship gives full control over its navigation to the pilot. In writing to the believers at Ephesus the apostle Paul says: "Do not get drunk with wine, for that is debauchery; but be filled with the Spirit" (Eph. 5:18). The tense in the Greek indicates this is not a once-for-all experience as was the Spirit baptism spoken of in 1 Corinthians 12:13. Rather, this is a repetitive experience meaning, "Keep on being filled." The passive voice indicates someone else must fill us. This is God's work in response to our willingness.

Paul's desire for the Ephesians—as for all followers of Jesus—is not an arbitrary command; rather, it is something within the believer's own choice, which the apostle hopes his converts will choose to comply with. His hope for them is that they be filled with the Spirit and be ruled, dominated, under His supreme direction, even as a drunkard, intoxicated with wine, is dominated or ruled by his intoxication. "Our Lord Himself has given the command, 'Be filled with the Spirit' (Ephesians 5:18), and this command is also a promise of its fulfillment."[9]

But there are prerequisites for the infilling of the fullness of the Holy Spirit. Here I shall only mention a few of them. First, individually we must be vitally interested in being filled with the Holy Spirit. We must hunger and thirst for Him. Does the following statement by the servant of the Lord possibly find its application in our experience? "The promise is not appreciated as it should be; and therefore its fulfillment is not seen as it might be. The promise of the Spirit is a matter little thought of."[10]

In most instances God wants you and me to have all the good things the heart longs for. But do we limit our requests to temporal blessings? He who asks only for material blessings is requesting only trifles from the Eternal One. Jesus said, "Seek first his kingdom and his righteousness, and all these things shall be yours as well" (Matt. 6:33). The Jews of old were eager to see God's promises to them as a nation fulfilled (see Deut. 28:1-14), but they sought primarily the fulfillment of secondary promises, rather than seeking "first his kingdom and his righteousness." Thus they never attained to God's ideal for them. Are we possibly like the Jews of old? How earnestly do you and I really desire and long for the fullness of the Holy Spirit?

As far back as I can recall, I have cherished a desire to be able to play the piano. When I was growing up, we had an instrument at home, but I can never recall putting my fingers on the keys. One of my brothers learned to play, and some of my sisters did also. The first time I tried to play the piano was when our oldest daughter, as a preschool girl of five or six years of age, dragged me to the piano and insisted that I learn to play "Peter, Peter, Pumpkin Eater." Since that time, I cannot recall having placed my fingers on the keys of the piano. With only such a lackadaisical desire to learn to play the piano, how soon could I really expect to be able to do so? Obviously never!

Is your desire and mine for the reception of the fullness of the Spirit just as languid as that?

If we desire anything more than to be filled with the Holy Spirit, then the blessed experience will not be ours. Furthermore, if we desire something else equally ardently, then the experience will not be granted us.

Second, we must claim the promise of the Holy Spirit by expecting to see it fulfilled in our personal experience. The disciples did that. Each one of them expected personally to receive the promised Holy Spirit. And as they unhesitatingly expected to see that promise of the Master fulfilled, they made preparation for it.

In anticipation of the arrival of our first baby, we procured a bassinet, baby bottles, and other necessary articles. My wife had her suitcase packed for weeks, ready to go to the hospital at the first indication that the baby's arrival was imminent. She needed only to pick it up and depart for the hospital. Our faith and expectation for the baby's arrival was real. It was as tangible as baby bottles and diapers. The disciples' expectation for the reception of the Holy Spirit was just as firm and real. Is your expectation and mine for the reception of the fullness of the Holy Spirit equally tangible?

Third, in order to be filled with the Holy Spirit we must follow the promptings of the Holy Spirit to the extent that you and I as Christians know Him today. And that means more than paying tithe, keeping the Sabbath, and attending church regularly. These things we will want to do. But to follow the promptings of the Holy Spirit means more. One day the Holy Spirit may whisper to you, "Go and speak a word of courage to Mr. Smith because he is discouraged." Or He may say to you, "Tell Mrs. Gray that you are sorry for what you said to her yesterday." In such a way the promptings of the Holy Spirit may come to your heart and mine daily. No one knows anything about these admonitions of the Holy Spirit except you and me ourselves.

Canvassing in a lumber region under the midnight sun in northern Sweden years ago, I systematically visited the homes and offices of a small lumber town, street by street, house after house, and business place after business place. But I purposely bypassed the office of a big lumber company for several days.

Every morning before! went to work, I heard a voice saying to me, "Go to the office of the lumber company today." But I refused. When I returned to my rented room in the evening, the voice was there again, saying, "Tomorrow morning, you go to the office of the lumber company." But I would not heed the voice that spoke to me. That office had many employees, some thirty men and women seated at their desks in a spacious room. To see the president of the company I would have to go through this large office. His desk was at the far end. Then I would have to present my sales talk to him in the sight and hearing of all those clerks. That I just did not want to do. But that inner voice did not leave me. Finally, I did go there, and what a burden rolled from my heart!

In a similar manner the Holy Spirit is speaking to us today. In order to be filled with the Spirit we must follow His promptings as we know Him today.

Fourth, in order to be filled with the Holy Spirit we must be undivided in our allegiance to God. You who are married may return in your thoughts to those blissful, dreamy days when you were courting your sweetheart. You men, relive the very evening you asked her to marry you. Imagine that this had been her reply as you asked her to marry you, "I like you a great deal, but I also like your friend Frank quite well." As she noticed you freezing up at this confession, she added quickly: "Although I promise to marry you, now and then I want to spend an evening with Frank."

What would you have done if she had answered you in that way? Would you have said, "I certainly appreciate your readiness to marry me"? No one of you would have married a girl like that and then given her your name, handed over to her your car keys, your billfold, and your checkbook. Irrespective of how much you loved her and how much you desired to marry her, you would not have dared to marry a girl who gave that answer to your marriage proposal.

If you and I were that particular about whom we married and to whom we gave access to our paltry possessions, should not God be particular as to whom He fills with the Holy Spirit? The Holy Spirit is the key to all the resources of the universe. "All 'good things' are comprised in this. The Creator Himself can give us nothing greater, nothing better."[11]

There can be no personal Pentecost or in filling of the fullness of the Holy Spirit without a personal Calvary. Jesus' way to victory lay through the cross. On Calvary's tree Jesus sealed His full and complete allegiance to His Father's will and to the glory of His kingdom. Without the historical Calvary there could have been no historical Pentecost. Likewise, unless there is a personal or experiential Calvary, there will be no experiential Pentecost. Only as we crucify all self-interest can we receive the fullness of the milling of the Holy Spirit. "When one is fully emptied of self, . . . the vacuum is filled by the inflowing of the Spirit of Christ."[12]

Why are we not filled with the Spirit? Probably it is because we have made little room for Him in our lives. "Minor matters occupy the attention, and the divine power which is necessary for the growth and prosperity of the church, and which would bring all other blessings in its train, is lacking, though offered in its infinite plenitude."[13] Today as in days of yore God is eagerly looking for men and women whose hearts are fully emptied of self and perfectly His. "The eyes of the Lord run to and fro throughout the whole earth, to show his might in behalf of those whose heart is blameless toward him" (2 Chron. 16:9). God does not merely want us to be baptized with the Spirit; He wants you and me to be filled with the Holy Spirit.

---

[1] Ellen G. White, *The Desire of Ages,* p. 176.
[2] *Ibid.,* p. 671.
[3] Ellen G. White, *Review and Herald,* Jan. 17, 1893.

[4] Ellen G. White, *Patriarchs and Prophets* (Mountain View, Calif.: Pacific Press Pub. Assn., 1890), pp. 632, 633.

[5] Ellen G. White, *Testimonies,* vol. 5, p. 278.

[6] Ellen G. White, *Review and Herald,* Jan. 24, 1893.

[7] Ellen G. White, *Christ's Object Lessons,* p. 139.

[8] Ellen G. White, *Thoughts From the Mount of Blessing* (Washington, D.C.: Review and Herald Pub. Assn., 1956), p. 21.

[9] *Ibid.*

[10] Ellen G. White, *Testimonies,* vol. 8, p. 21.

[11] Ellen G. White, *Thoughts From the Mount of Blessing,* p. 132.

[12] Ellen G. White, *Gospel Workers* (Washington, D.C.: Review and Herald Pub. Assn., 1915), p. 287.

[13] Ellen G. White, *Testimonies,* vol. 8, p. 21.

CHAPTER 7

The Manifestations
of the Spirit

The Spirit is one, but His gifts or manifestations are many, diverse, and distinct. These gifts of grace, or *charismata,* as they are called (transliterated from the original Greek), are presented in three different passages in the Bible: Romans 12:4-8; 1 Corinthians 12-14; and Ephesians 4:8-13. Probably even these three passages are not exhaustive, but are rather illustrative of possible spiritual endowments.

The gifts mentioned in the three Bible passages cannot always be clearly differentiated. Some of them spill over their boundaries and have characteristics common with another. These gifts were vouchsafed to the church in a special way when Jesus ascended to heaven. About them the apostle Paul says, " 'When he ascended on high he led a host of captives, and he gave gifts to men.' . . . And his gifts were that some should be apostles, some prophets, some evangelists, some pastors and teachers" (Eph. 4:8-11).

These gifts or manifestations of the Spirit should be differentiated from the fruit of the Spirit presented in Galatians 5:22, 23. Every Christian should expect to see all the different facets of the fruit of the Spirit gradually appear in his life, but he should not expect to receive all the different gifts or manifestations of the Spirit.

The apostle Paul compares the church to a body. Through the Spirit we were all born again and became members of the body of Christ as we gave our lives to God and joined a local church through baptism. "Just as the body is one and has many members, and all the members of the body, though many, are one body, so it is with Christ. For by one Spirit we were all baptized into one body—Jews or Greeks, slaves or free—and all were made to drink of one Spirit." "Now you are the body of Christ and individually members of it" (1 Cor. 12:12, 13, 27).

The members of the body of Christ, or of the church, are no more

MANIFESTATIONS OF THE SPIRIT			
RSV	Rom. 12:5-8	1 Cor. 12 to 14	Eph. 4:8-13
Prophecy	X	X	X
Service—ternporal and external: ministry; "Dorcas" matters for poor, sick, stranger	X		
Teaching	X	X	X
Exhortation (encouragement, consolation)	X		
Giving—contributing, sharing one's own	X		
Ruling (KJV)—giving aid	X		
Showing mercy	X		
Wisdom		X	
Knowledge		X	
Faith		X	
Healing		X	
Miracles		X	
Discerning of spirits			
Tongues		X	
Tongues—interpretation		X	
Apostles		X	X
Helpers		X	
Administrators governments		X	
Evangelists			X
Pastors			X

alike than the five digits of the hand or the different members or organs of the body. Nevertheless, they are all part of the same hand or body. As such they cooperate or work together in harmony. All the members of the hand or the body belong to the same body and serve a very definite purpose in it. Neither the hand nor the body will be complete or even constitute a hand or a body without all the different members.

The gifts or manifestations of the Spirit are represented by the different members in the church. No church member should expect to receive them all. This would be as unnatural as if one organ of the human body would be able to perform all the functions of all the other organs or parts of the body. Neither should all the members of the church expect to receive the same and identical gift or gifts. If the whole human body would constitute but one organ, there would be no body, but a monstrosity. And Jesus likens the church, in which the manifestations of the Spirit appear, to the human body.

As all the different organs and limbs in the human body together compose the body, so all the different gifts of the Spirit will be found in different members and together make up the church. This is the case in the human body. Still, one organ does not look down upon another organ and tell it that it must be like the first organ, or that the other organ is of no importance or is unnecessary. Rather, in a healthy body the different organs or parts work together harmoniously and function as a unit.

Christ gave these gifts to the church "to equip the saints for the work of ministry, for building up the body of Christ, until we all attain to the unity of the faith and of the knowledge of the Son of God, to mature manhood, to the measure of the stature of the fullness of Christ" (Eph. 4:12, 13).

Of the gifts mentioned by Paul only two are mentioned in each of the three passages where he discusses the *charismata*. These two are prophecy and teaching. "Apostles" is mentioned in two of the passages. All the others are mentioned in only one of the three passages.

Prophecy. As a prophet is primarily a spokesman for God, or a forthteller rather than a foreteller, so prophecy is mainly *forthtelling* rather than foretelling. A better translation of prophecy would simply be preaching. God unveils His will and plans to the prophet, and the prophet conveys God's messages to the people.

Moses, the wise and renowned leader of Israel during the Exodus, was a great prophet. But a very small portion of Moses' writings consists of predictions. Rather, he gave the messages God wanted him to convey to His people. These consisted of instruction, warnings, advice, and guidance needed by His people. John the Baptist was the greatest born of woman and a prophet (see Matt. 11:11; Luke 7:28). He was a spokesman for God, giving His designed messages to His people.

Service. The King James Version calls it ministry. But service and ministry in the original meaning are actually the same. The word in the original denotes all kinds of ministry in the church. But as it here stands in relation to other gifts of the Spirit, it probably refers to help given to the poor, the sick, and the strangers. It possibly covers the service mentioned by Jesus as having been fulfilled by those on His right hand in the parable of the judgment in Matthew 25:35, 36.

Teaching. This gift of the Spirit is more than pedagogical skill in the communication of knowledge. It probably includes this but is more importantly the ability to awaken an understanding of God and His will in sinners. It refers to the wisdom possessed by the wise spoken of by the prophet Daniel "who have taught many people to do what is right" (Dan. 12:3, TEV).

Exhortation. This gift implies an encouragement or coming to someone's help. The word used is akin to *paraclete*. It is indeed a gift of the Spirit to be able to build up people who are sagging under discouragement and the cares of life. Jesus verily did this with the woman taken in adultery (see John 8:1-11). Isaiah says of Him: "A bruised reed he will not break, and a dimly burning wick he will not quench" (Isa. 42:3). Such will also be the ministry of those who are granted this gift by the Spirit.

Giving. The gift of giving is not based on a socialistic philosophy that all members of society will do their best work to give their surplus earnings to those who cannot meet their needs. Charismatic giving is rather based on one's sense of stewardship under God, recognizing that the means I have accumulated I hold in trust under God. I do not own my possessions; rather, I owe them to the great Giver, for "you shall remember the Lord your God, for it is he who gives you power to get wealth" (Deut. 8:18).

But money or possessions are not the only gifts we may share with others. One of the most valuable gifts is time. Am I willing to give some of my time to God's saints and others who may be confined to a bed? Do I visit the elderly who seldom receive a visit from anyone? Such people deeply treasure the gift of time you are willing to give them. Such giving is a manifestation of the Spirit.

Ruling. "He that ruleth, with diligence" (KJV). "He who gives aid, with zeal" (RSV). "Whoever has authority should work hard" (TEV). Barclay translates this phrase: "If we are called upon to supply leadership, let us do so with zeal." In other words, if we are called to leadership, we should discharge our responsibility with zeal. Paul means that we should not discharge our responsibility reluctantly, but enter into our tasks willingly and energetically.

It is possible to fill an office and merely go through the motions of service, particularly if the service rendered is gratuitous. If we have accepted the position—and we should if called upon to do so—we should engage in the work with joy and thrill with zeal as we labor in love.

Showing Mercy. When mercy is shown, it should be done with cheerfulness and kindness, Paul says. Mercy may be rendered with an attitude that hurts and demoralizes. Jesus, in contrast to the hardness of the Jews, showed mercy toward the woman taken in adultery. He did the same for Mary Magdalene, who anointed His feet with oil at Simon the leper's house (see Luke 7:36-50). He did it in such a way that it lifted Mary, the sinner, and made her into a new person despite her past sinful life. It prompted Mary to linger long at the cross and arrive first at the grave of Jesus on the resurrection morning.

Wisdom. The wisdom the apostle apparently speaks about among the gifts of the Spirit is a saving acquaintance with the plan of salvation. This is how he identifies wisdom in 1 Corinthians 2:7. Another interesting text with the same meaning is Daniel 12:3. This wisdom is saving insight into the plan of God and a personal acquaintance with Jesus.

Knowledge. Paul uses the word knowledge in its traditional Hebrew meaning of obedient acknowledgment of God's will. Its meaning was distinct from what we often term theoretical knowledge. Rather, it was applied knowledge. This is indeed knowledge by the grace of God.

Faith. Personal faith or trust in God is initially a gift of God. Paul says so in Romans 12:3. Ellen White lists it, along with other gifts of the Spirit, as a talent.[1] As such it is to be invested and traded so that the initial capital may grow. The faithful stewards of Matthew 25 doubled their initial capital. We as Christians will use our faith, or trust in God, until we take His word at face value. When we come to that place in our relationship to God, then we shall know "that He loves us and knows best what is for our good. Thus, instead of our own, it leads us to choose His way."[2]

Healing. Healing—physical, emotional, mental—is a gift of God. It is God's wish that we be in good health. The apostle John prayed for the believers that they might "be in health" (3 John 2). Ultimately sickness is a result of sin, although not necessarily of personal sin. This Jesus made crystal clear when the disciples queried Him as to whose fault it was that a man had been born blind (see John 9:1-3). But sickness, in all its forms, is a result of the cumulative sins of man.

Discerning of Spirits. There are different spirits (see 1 John 4:1). Some are good, or emanate from God; others are evil and are servants of Satan. It is a gift of God to be able to discern the spirits and their origin. The eye-salve of the Spirit will enable the believer to identify any particular spirit as to whose servant he is.

Apostles. We do not believe that this gift of apostleship must be limited to the twelve. James was also called an apostle (see 1 Cor. 15:7; Gal. 1:19). And Paul called himself apostle. Yet these men had not been part of the twelve while Jesus was with them (see Acts 1:21, 22). An apostle literally is one sent out, or a missionary. We would possibly apply the designation to a person who has general leadership responsibility over the church universal. In this way we could apply the term apostle to the officers of the General Conference, with their responsibilities to the world church.

Helpers. The gift of being "helpers" may seem to be very lowly and hence unimportant. Still, it is listed as being one of the gifts of the Spirit to the church body. The small toe may appear to be of minor importance as part of the human body. I have a friend who lost one of his small toes. The absence of this small or apparently very insignificant part of the total body causes a slight limp in his gait and makes it impossible for him to run. The small toe is essential to give balance to the human body.

In the same way "helpers" are necessary in the church to perform the office of the deacon and to minister to the poor and the sick. Skills of designing and building, mechanical abilities, agricultural expertise—these and many more "helps" make God's work prosper. This work gains little or no recognition. Nevertheless, it is indispensable in order that the church may reflect the ministry and solicitude of Jesus for the minor details of life and care for the forgotten and neglected. Jesus did give attention to details; He took time to fold His graveclothes before He went out of the tomb on the resurrection morning. On another occasion he was also mindful of a seemingly worthless human derelict whom self-righteous bigots wanted to stone (see John 8:1-11).

Administrators. The gospel and its proclamation is ultimately God's work. But God has committed it to men. Someone must oversee and direct the work.

A certain legend says that on His return to heaven Jesus called the angels together and told them about His mission and the provision He had made for the completion of the work He had begun on earth. When they learned that He had left it all with eleven men, they asked him with forebodings, "Did you not make any other plans?"

"No," their returned Ruler replied, "I am depending on my eleven remaining disciples."

Today, Jesus is still depending on His followers on earth to complete the unfinished task. And the administrators are directing the armies of modern Israel in this work.

Evangelists. According to the literal translation from the Greek these were preachers of the gospel. Apparently they were not confined to a specific locality as the pastors, but were missionaries to the unconverted. They would move from place to place as they found openings for the proclamation of the gospel. In a sense these too are counterparts to our missionaries.

Pastors. In Ephesians 4:11 pastors and teachers are coupled together suggesting two phases of one kind of ministry. Teaching is one part of an effective pastoral ministry. Jesus Himself was a prototype of a true pastor. He taught His disciples as He shepherded them. By following His example the pastor will make his work fruit-bearing.

★ ★ ★

As each organ or limb in the human body has its own specific function, so each member in Christ's body, the church, has his special work. "Not more surely is the place prepared for us in the heavenly mansions than is the special place designated on earth where we are to work for God."[3]

One member of the church should not disdain, or envy, another member who has received a different gift. "There are different ways of serving, but the same Lord is served. There are different abilities to perform service, but the same God gives ability to everyone for his particular service. The Spirit's presence is shown in some way in each person for the good of all" (1 Cor. 12:5-7, TEV).

In manufacturing articles of any kind, utilities, cars, etc., manufacturers, or producers, tend to make all the articles or products alike. It is easier for man to do this than to make them all different. God, on the other hand, makes no two things alike. Of the thousands of leaves on a tree, the botanist tells us that every leaf is different. Of the untold millions or billions of snow crystals beautifying the snowscape on a crisp, moonlit winter night, no two are alike. Nor are the fingerprints on the billions of people in the world. They are all different. God uses no assembly lines. His mind is sufficiently fertile to make things different. Man, on the other hand, prefers the assembly line because of his lack of imagination or fertility of mind or because he wants to reduce the cost of production. God is limited neither by lack of ideas nor prohibitive costs. He is both sufficiently wise and rich to make things different.

On a small scale God follows this pattern in His dealings with His church. He does not give all members the same gifts; He gives them different gifts, by the same Spirit. Every member in the church is a person and is indeed unique—he has no complete replica.

Without a doubt we as Christians have circumscribed the manifestations of the Spirit too narrowly. It would be well for us as Seventhday Adventists in particular to recognize that the gifts of God and the manifestations of the Spirit are just as verily manifested in the work or the skill of the hands as in intellectual gifts like teaching, writing, or speaking. The Spirit imparted manual dexterity to Bezaleel so that he was enabled to produce all the art work for the sanctuary (see Ex. 35:30-35). Likewise Dr. Kellogg received along with medical knowledge manual dexterity and ability to perform delicate surgical operations.[4] In the same way the mechanic, the carpenter, and other craftsmen received their peculiar gift from God. The mother in the kitchen and others who engage in food preparation have likewise a gift from God, since "there is more religion in a loaf of good bread than many think." Furthermore "souls are lost as the result of poor cookery."[5] Another gift or manifestation of the Spirit is the ability to make money or "power to get wealth" (Deut. 8:18). God gives to each person a gift or a skill to use.

After having enumerated many different manifestations of the Spirit in 1 Corinthians 12, the apostle concludes by saying in verse 31, "Earnestly desire the higher gifts. And I will show you a still more excellent way." The manifestation par excellence of the Spirit is none of those already mentioned, but—love (see 1 Cor. 13). Love alone will make all these other gifts work together. Therefore "above all these put on love, which binds everything together in perfect harmony" (Col. 3:14). Love "is the burning—glass which unremittingly re-concentrates the diverse charismatic manifestations toward their unified goal"[6] of the common good of the church or the body of Christ.

"Christian unity is a mighty agency. It tells in a powerful manner that those who possess it are children of God. It has an irresistible influence upon the world. Showing that man in his humanity may be a partaker of the divine nature, having escaped the corruption that is in the world through lust. We are to be one with our fellow men and with Christ, and in Christ one with God. Then of us can be spoken the words, 'Ye are complete in Him.'"[7]

When the apostolic church thought back upon Jesus, He did not stand out in their memory as a superb administrator or organizer or even as an exceedingly intelligent and knowledgeable teacher, nor primarily as a superb speaker (although He was), but as One who "went about doing good" (Acts 10:38; compare Matt. 9:35). The reason or source for His goodness was the anointing of the Holy Spirit. Because of this, "from His earliest years He was possessed of one purpose; He lived to bless others."[8] "In the life of Christ, everything was made subordinate to His work, the great work of redemption which He came to accomplish."[9]

As we members of the church of God are recipients of the highest gift of the Spirit—love—we too will be animated by the same objective.

The Manifestation of Tongues

One of the manifestations of the Spirit is the use of different kinds of tongues (see 1 Cor. 12:10) or the ability "to speak in tongues." Reference to speaking in tongues is made in four different places in the New Testament. Three of these are found in the book of Acts; namely, in Acts chapters 2, 10, and 19. The other is in 1 Corinthians 12-14.

For tongue(s) in each instance the Greek work *glōssa(i)* is used. This Greek word means either the anatomical tongue or language.

There is no misunderstanding in connection with the speaking in tongues in Acts 2. There it is plainly stated that the people spoke in other languages. Several of these languages are mentioned. The apostles, and apparently the church members who were associated with them on the Day of Pentecost, miraculously received, through the Holy Spirit, the ability to speak fluently languages which they had never learned. The Holy Spirit did for them that which they could not have accomplished for themselves in a lifetime."[10]

Having been filled with the Holy Spirit on the Day of Pentecost, the early Christians cherished a desire to communicate the message of salvation to those who knew it not. This desire animated the whole group of believers. They wanted to tell all the visiting Jews from the Diaspora, now assembled at Jerusalem for the Passover Feast, the wondrous story of Jesus and His love; how He had come down to this earth and suffered and died that every human being who was willing might be saved through His shed blood. But they could not readily do this, handicapped as they were by the inability to speak the languages represented by these strangers now present in Jerusalem. But God Himself miraculously intervened to remove this obstacle to the spread of the gospel.

As the Holy Spirit descended upon the believers in the form of tongues of fire, the language barriers curtailing their gospel proclamation were swept away. Suddenly the Christians were able to speak fluently the languages represented by the numerous visitors at the feast.

Apparently the different apostles, as well as other believers, initially spoke to different groups in different languages. As the Christians spoke these different languages, the people heard their own languages spoken. As the climax to the day's activities, Peter delivered a message to all the people.

The other instances of speaking in tongues in the book of Acts refer to occasions when Peter or Paul was preaching. At these times the Holy Spirit fell on new believers at Caesarea under the preaching of the apostle Peter (see Acts 10:44), and on the believers at Ephesus under the preaching of Paul (see Acts 19:6). In both cases, the manifestation of the Holy Spirit was accompanied by the gift of speaking other languages, just as had been the case on the Day of Pentecost. Again, the endowment of the gift of tongues was for the rapid proclamation of the gospel.

Undoubtedly, people of different languages lived in the port town of Caesarea. Here a command of other languages would be a means of facilitating the spread of the story of salvation. Ephesus was a commercial city and a busy port. Many people from other countries lived there also. These people could be reached with the gospel through missionaries who knew their languages.

The last instance where the speaking in tongues is mentioned in the New Testament is in 1 Corinthians 12 to 14. This instance is more puzzling than the occurrences of it recorded in the book of Acts. The word "unknown," inserted in the King James Version before tongue(s) (italicized in some editions), contributes to the confusion. "Unknown" is not found in the original Greek but is inserted. The original says only that they spoke in tongues, or in languages, as the phrase might more accurately be translated.

In verse 2 of 1 Corinthians 14 it says that those who spoke in tongues at Corinth did not speak unto men but unto God. They spoke mysteries; no one could understand them. Consequently, the speaker edified only himself by speaking in tongues (verse 4). Nevertheless, Paul wishes that more of the church members might speak in tongues (verse 5), although the speaking in tongues did not profit the hearers (verses 5, 6, and 17). In verse 14 Paul states that the individual who spoke in tongues spoke with his spirit rather than with his understanding. Consequently, his understanding was unfruitful. An unlearned person was therefore unable to thank God for what was being said because he could not understand. Paul himself spoke in tongues more than anyone else in the Corinthian church (verse 18). Still, he would rather speak five words with his understanding than 10,000 words in a tongue (verse 19).

Tongue speaking, Paul says, was a sign to unbelievers (verse 22). At the same time, unbelievers and unlearned people believed that speaking in tongues which they could not understand was a sign of madness (verse 23).

Paul advises the Corinthian church that if they were to continue to speak in tongues, only two or three should do so in sequence, and the tongues must be interpreted (verse 27). If no interpreter is present, no one should speak in tongues (verses 13 and 28), since it created confusion (verse 33). Nevertheless, the speaking in tongues was not to be forbidden (verse 39), but it should be done in an orderly fashion.

Many different interpretations have been given of the speaking in tongues at Corinth, as recorded in 1 Corinthians 14. Many commentators believe that the Christians in the Corinthian church indulged in ecstatic speech that no one understood, not even the speakers themselves, and that this ecstatic speaking denoted a high or elevated experience with God. I know one man who claims that he has not merely spoken in tongues but has also sung in tongues. He admits that he did not understand the words that he was speaking and singing but that it gave him a feeling of elation and indescribable happiness.

Corinth was a seaport. People of all nationalities were assembled in this port city, as they are in New York and other big seaports throughout the world. Many of these foreigners in Corinth had been brought into the church of Jesus Christ. They belonged to the Christian church which was markedly cosmopolitan. But having come from other parts of the Roman Empire, they were not all fluent in the Greek language. Thus they preferred to speak their own languages because they could express themselves more fluently and easily in them than in Greek.

When this cosmopolitan group met for their church services, some were prone to express themselves in their own native languages. In a social service or a testimony meeting, a man from a far corner of the Roman Empire would start speaking in his own language that hardly anyone else in the congregation understood. Consequently, he did not speak unto men. He spoke unto God, as Paul says in verse 2. As far as the other believers were concerned, he spoke mysteries, and no one understood him (verses 2, 9). His fellow believers were not edified by what he said, since it was incomprehensible to them; he edified only himself.

Paul wished that all might be able to speak different languages (verse 5). Such gifts could be a means of reaching other people who also used those languages. But naturally it did not profit the believers who did not understand (verses 5, 6, 17).

Paul says that he himself spoke languages more than anyone else. He had probably grown up speaking Aramaic in his Jewish home in the city of Tarsus in Cilicia. This was the language common among the Jews in Palestine in the days of Jesus. But Paul had also learned the Greek language. He was at least bilingual. Possibly he also knew some Latin since Tarsus was a city with strong Roman influence. After all, the government was in the hands of the Romans, and probably many Roman officials preferred to speak Latin. He undoubtedly also knew Hebrew, the language used in the synagogues.

In his evangelism throughout the Roman Empire, Paul started out by visiting the Jewish synagogues in each location. This he did when he first landed in Macedonia. In the synagogues he undoubtedly spoke Aramaic to the people, and possibly some Hebrew to the scribes and the synagogue officers. But when he left the Jewish synagogues, he was forced to leave the Aramaic and Hebrew languages behind, the Gentiles not being able to understand either language. In such instances he undoubtedly resorted to Greek. In this language he could reach large Gentile crowds. In his proclamation of the gospel he invariably had to use a language which was different from his native Aramaic when he became the apostle unto the Gentiles. And so he could confidently say that he spoke in tongues or other languages more than in his own native language, and more than anyone else even in the Corinthian church (verse 18).

Paul says that the speaking in tongues was a sign to the unbelievers (verse 22). This had truly been the case on the Day of Pentecost. When the strangers from all parts of the Roman Empire heard the apostles and the early Christians speak in their own provincial languages on the Day of Pentecost, then they understood that this was a direct miracle from God. Thus speaking in tongues was a sign to the unbelievers. They were compelled to acknowledge that this was an indication that the proclaimers of the gospel were indeed the servants of the most high God. God Himself gave them ability to speak languages that they had never learned. Their mastery of them became a sign to the unbelievers that the power of God was manifested.

But when an unbeliever came into the Corinthian Christian church and found two or three, or even four, speaking different languages at the same time in the same room, these unbelievers said that the Christians were crazy or mad (verse 23). Naturally so, since the congregation would appear, particularly since no one interpreted, like a madhouse. Consequently, Paul advised that only two or three should speak, at the most, and these in sequence (verse 27).

It was good for these people who did not have a perfect command of the Greek language to speak to the glory of God in their own languages. It was better for them to do this than to be silent all the time, but an interpreter should be present when it was done in the church so that it might be translated and made comprehensible to the other believers also, who did not understand the particular language spoken. If this was not done, the speaking in tongues was a cause of utter confusion (verse 33). Nevertheless, Paul says that the speaking in tongues should not be forbidden (verse 39).

It would be easy for us as Seventh-day Adventists with people present from all parts of the world at an Annual Council or at a General Conference session to reproduce the scene presented in the Corinthian church. Many of those in attendance at the General Conference session in Vienna in 1975 would have felt freer to speak in another language than in English or German. Imagine that all those delegates to the General Conference had started to speak each in his own language and at the same time. What a madhouse that would have made out of the Stadthalle, or the meeting place.

Verse 14 in the King James Version has particularly puzzled many. It says, "For if I pray in an unknown tongue, my spirit prayeth, but my understanding is unfruitful." This might give the impression that the praying in a tongue was indeed only ecstatic babbling.

In the story of the unfruitful fig tree in Matthew 21:19, Jesus pronounced a curse on the tree by saying, "May no fruit ever come from you again." This same Greek root for fruit is used in 1 Corinthians 14:14, and the Revised Standard Version translates the phrase, "My spirit prays but my mind is unfruitful." Luther translates this phrase in the same way: "mein Sinn bring niemand Frucht." The Swedish translation of 1917 reads in the same way: "mitt förstånd kommer ingen frukt åstad." William F. Arndt and F. Wilbur Gingrich in *A Greek-English Lexicon of the New Testament* translate this phrase in 1 Corinthians 14:14 "my mind is unproductive."[11]

There is a difference between being without intelligence and being unfruitful or not producing fruit. The speech of those who spoke in tongues in the Corinthian church was not without intelligence. They spoke with intelligence and understood what they said; but, in spite of that, their speaking and praying in tongues produced no fruit—found no response in the minds and the hearts of those who heard it—because the hearers failed to understand. So Paul says in verse 17: "For you may give thanks well enough, but the other man is not edified," because he does not understand.

Further proof that tongues in 1 Corinthians 14 refers to intelligent languages is found in verse 21. Here Paul quotes an Old Testament passage referring to a foreign language and speaks of it as tongues *(glōssai)*. Consequently, his use of the word *glōssa(i)* throughout the entire chapter logically must have the same meaning.

Tongues were a gift of the Spirit at Pentecost, given specifically for the proclamation of the gospel to the non-Aramaic-speaking Jews from all parts of the Roman Empire.

It was a gift given for the benefit of the unbelievers (verse 22) attending the feast. These could be reached only through these tongues or languages that the Spirit enabled the Jerusalem believers to use. The use of tongues was indeed a sign to unbelievers on the Day of Pentecost. Foreigners were convinced that the apostles were God's messengers when God enabled them to speak their particular languages. But Paul admonished that in the church one ought to prophesy, or proclaim God's message in a language known to the people (verse 22), rather than speak in tongues or languages that no one understood.

Paul exhorted the Corinthian believers that they strive for *the best* manifestation of the Spirit. That is love, he points out in 1 Corinthians 13:13-14:2. The greatest one of them would manifest this gift of the Spirit most fully.

But apparently some of the Corinthian believers, by using tongues or languages, had tried to impress the others that they possessed the Spirit. On the Day of Pentecost God Himself had separated those who possessed the Spirit from those who did not, by giving those who were filled with the Spirit the mastery of other languages. In a church split into factions by dissension, as was the Corinthian church, some who knew other languages tried to flaunt their alleged gift of the Spirit by using these languages in the congregational worship. Several of these exhibitionists would even speak at the same time without any interpreter.

This practice or bedlam Paul condemns, although he does not rule out the gift of tongues. Rather, he wished that all could speak in some other language besides his own native tongue. Then they all could reach certain strangers in the city.

Even today some members in the Christian community think that in order to be a Christian at all one must possess the gift of "tongues," or must have "spoken in tongues." If one does not have the gift of "tongues," they claim, he does not know Christ as his Savior. The apostle Paul decisively rules out such an overbearing attitude by rhetorically asking, "Do all work miracles? Do all possess gifts of healing? Do all speak with tongues? Do all interpret?" (1 Cor. 12:29, 30). The answer obviously is "No." He further says, "To each is given the manifestation of the Spirit for the common good" (1 Cor. 12:7). The Spirit was not to cause confusion and division in the church, for the supreme gift of the Spirit is love.

The Manifestation of Miracles

"The working of miracles" or the demonstration of mighty powers is indissolubly connected with the work of God. It is one of the manifestations of the Spirit (see 1 Cor. 12:10). God Himself is a miracle worker. To man many of His mighty acts are miracles, lying beyond human comprehension. He also entrusts His followers with the power to work miracles.

Moses was a worker of miracles. His commission to lead the children of Israel out of Egypt was accompanied and confirmed by miracles. But to begin with, the magicians of Egypt duplicated Moses' every miracle, though these were performed at the direct command of God. The magicians too turned rods into serpents; they turned the waters of the Nile into blood; they called forth frogs (see Ex. 7, 8). Finally Moses stood forth as the unchallenged servant of God before the magicians of Egypt, since the magicians no longer could match his miracles. The magicians themselves pointed to his miracles as conclusive evidence and validation of his divine ambassadorship.

We remember the prophet Elijah, the loyal servant of the true God in the time of King Ahab. On Mount Carmel he called down fire from heaven. This proved to the wavering Israelites that he was indeed the servant of the God of heaven; the prophets of Baal were discredited because they failed to match his feat (see 1 Kings 18:24, 37-39). Elisha was a miracle worker par excellence. He wrought healings and even a resurrection from the dead.

Jesus was a worker of miracles. Often He pointed to His mighty works, or appealed to His miracles, as evidence of His divine authority and Messiahship. In John 5:36 He says: "The testimony which I have is greater than that of John; for the works which the Father has granted me to accomplish, these very works which I am doing, bear me witness that the Father has sent me." In John 10:25 He says: "The works that I do in my Father's name, they bear witness of me." And again: "If I am not doing the works of my Father, then do not believe me; but if I do them, even though you do not believe me, believe the works, that you may know and understand that the Father is in me and I in the Father" (John 10:37, 38). Sincere men did recognize divinity operating in Jesus through His works.

At the first Passover during Jesus' public ministry "many believed in his name, when they saw the signs which he did" (John 2:23). Nicodemus recognized Jesus as a teacher sent from God, because of the miracles He performed. He confessed, "No one can do these signs that you do, unless God is with him" (John 3:2).

Many, like Nicodemus, were impressed by the signs. A multitude followed him [Jesus], because they saw the signs which he did on those who were diseased" (John 6:2).

Others questioned: "How can a man who is a sinner do such signs?" (John 9:16). To these men, as to the multitudes, His miracles validated His claim to be servant of the true God.

Miracles also accompanied the preaching of the post-Pentecostal Christians. Peter and John healed a lame man at the Temple (see Acts 3:1-11). Peter healed the paralytic Aeneas at Lydda and raised Dorcas from the dead at Joppa (see Acts 9:32-41). Paul raised young Eutychus from the dead (see Acts 20:9, 10).

Contemporaries of the apostles and early Christians believed that they possessed healing power. "They even carried out the sick into the streets, and laid them on beds and pallets, that as Peter came by at least his shadow might fall on some of them" (Acts 5:15). Luke records this of Paul's ministry at Ephesus: "God did extraordinary miracles by the hands of Paul, so that handkerchiefs or aprons were carried away from his body to the sick, and diseases left them and the evil spirits came out of them" (Acts 19:11, 12). Of Philip the record says that "the multitudes with one accord gave heed to what was said by Philip, when they heard him and saw the signs which he did" (Acts 8:6).

The miracle ministry of the early Christians is summed up in Hebrews 2:4 which reads: "God . . . bore witness by signs and wonders and various miracles and by gifts of the Holy Spirit distributed according to his own will (see also Rom. 15:18, 19; 2 Cor. 12:12).

In the end time one prominent manifestation of the Spirit will again be the working of miracles. In harmony with the best biblical pattern it will be convincingly argued that only servants of the true God can perform miracles. The question therefore arises, Are miracles inseparable accompaniments and irrefutable evidence of the divine ambassadorship of the person who performs them, and do miracles thus validate his religious teachings as originating with God?

The other day an acquaintance of mine told me of a definite miracle of healing. Then she wonderingly queried if I did not think that the person who performed such a miracle must be a loyal servant of the true God. Her supposition was that no one who did not serve God from a sincere heart could possibly be instrumental in performing such a miracle. Her reasoning was in harmony with the best tradition of biblical miracles.

Again we face the question raised in the days of Jesus, "How can a man who is a sinner do such miracles?" (John 9:16). The masses will be forced to agree with this conclusion: "We know that God does not listen to sinners, but if any one is a worshiper of God and does his will, God listens to him" (John 9:31). Again it will be argued, "If this man [who performs such miracles] were not from God, he could do nothing" (John 9:33). Jesus Himself said of His miracles: "The works that I do in my Father's name, they bear witness to me" (John 10:25).

Miracles will again become prominent. "Servants of God, with their faces lighted up and shining with holy consecration, will hasten from place to place to proclaim the message from heaven. By thousands of voices, all over the earth, the warning will be given. Miracles will be wrought, the sick will be healed, and signs and wonders will follow the believers."[12]

But the followers of the great apostate will also perform miracles. "Spirits of devils" (Rev. 16:14, KJV) will work miracles (see Matt. 24:24; Rev. 19:20). The miracles of Elijah on Mount Carmel will be reenacted, but this time by an apostate power (see Rev. 13:13). Satan himself shall perform lying wonders (see 2 Thess. 2:9). In doing this he will appear as an angel of light (see 2 Cor. 11:14). "He will continue these wonders [miracles of healing, etc.] until the close of probation, that he may point to them as evidence that he is an angel of light and not of darkness."[13] "These works of apparent healing will bring Seventh-day Adventists to the test."[14]

As in Bible times miracles will be looked upon as conclusive evidence that those who perform them must be the faithful followers and servants of the true God. This will indeed be a compelling argument.

So far, we as Seventh-day Adventists have often looked askance on reports of miraculous healings and are prone to regard all such reports as sleight-of-hand performances or the result of individual or mass hypnosis. I shall refrain from passing judgment on the "healings" of various faith healers of the past and also of the present. Whatever the case may have been in the past, and is at the present, I know that according to divine revelation genuine miracles of healing, as well as other miracles, will be performed in the future by subjects of another power who claim to be the servants of the true God.

The world at large will be deceived by these miracles. "Papists, who boast miracles as a certain sign of the true church, will be readily deceived by this wonder-working power [Satan working through spiritualism]; and Protestants, having cast away the shield of truth, will also be deluded.

Papists, Protestants, and worldlings will alike accept the form of godliness."[15] Although Satan cannot create or impart life, he can at times cause illness and then he can remove the cause of the illness which he himself has brought about and thus give the effect of virtual healing.

When both apostates and sincere followers of God perform miracles, it is evident that miracles in themselves cannot be looked upon as accompaniments and validation of the divine origin of their religious teachings. Ours is an age of science. But it is as susceptible to deception by miracles as were the Middle Ages, or the so-called age of faith. Science is empirical; it relies on observation and demonstration. Its method is experiment and observation. According to science all ideas should be capable of being verified or disproved by experiment or observation. They should be subject to reason and should conform to the laws of nature. Theory becomes dependent primarily upon systematic experiment. Indemonstrable hypotheses are readily rejected. In other words, nothing should be accepted unless it can be demonstrated.

Scientific philosophy or mode of thinking has penetrated and affected all areas of modern life. The scientific premise that everything should be demonstrable has also affected religious thinking. Christianity has never in the past encountered anything comparable to the impact of modern science. Christians are today compelled to face greater challenges to their basic beliefs than they faced during the Renaissance and the Reformation. Many therefore are convinced that man has outgrown religion altogether, because religion inevitably invokes the supernatural.

Never has Christian orthodoxy and faith in God been so severely challenged. Hence, the majority of people today stand outside the community of Christian faith. Many of them are intellectuals who wear a garment of agnosticism. They believe that the world expects them as intellectuals to wear it. Some young people are in this group. Others standing outside the Christian community are those reaping the new affluence. They are utterly absorbed in materialism and in the acquisition of creature comforts.

Disbelief in Christianity today is not due to ignorance. If enlightenment were a requisite for Christian faith, then Christianity would have entered its golden age. Many of those standing outside the Christian fold have critically evaluated and measured it and found it wanting. *Unfortunately, they have measured it with the wrong measure; namely, demonstration,* or the yardstick used by science. But some realities in life are not amenable to sense perception or demonstration. Science insists that everything must be amenable to demonstration or perceivable by the senses.

All personal life embraces subjective or personal factors. These personal factors are the very essence of intelligent life, and they reveal intelligent beings as they actually are. How do you prove love? A young lady answers, "I know he loves me because he cares for me and gives me candy and flowers." But that does not prove he loves you. He may give you those things because he loves himself or because he wants something from you in return. First Corinthians 13:3 reads, "If I give away all I have, and if I deliver my body to be burned, but have not love, I gain nothing."

Vital religion is a personal relationship of sacred intimacy between the person and God, like that between husband and wife. Therefore, it is useless for me to try intellectually to convince a skeptic of God's goodness. Further, an infidel is not converted by argument. For an infidel to believe in God and His goodness, he must personally become acquainted with God and then cease to be an infidel. In order to believe and trust God, he must know Him. Neither logic nor reason will convince him of God's existence and goodness apart from a personal acquaintance.

Often we think that miracles have no place in an enlightened, scientific age. In this way the Christian who still believes in miracles is an anachronism—he is not keeping pace with the times in which he lives. He believes there are powers outside of or superior to nature. As a supernaturalist he believes these emanate either from God or the devil.

Are miracles possible? Do they occur? So far, the scientific world has looked askance on miracles. If a rationalist sees a miracle, he explains it away. Jesus, after the resurrection, appeared to friends. There was no need to appear to His enemies; they would not believe in His resurrection anyway. Luke 16:31 states: "If they hear not Moses and the prophets, neither will they be persuaded, though one rose from the dead." Seeing is not necessarily believing.

But the miracles in the end-time will be so overwhelming that all will come to believe in their reality. People in this age of science will be convinced that there is life after death when they see their departed dead ones appear. But their presumed departed friends will be impersonated by evil spirits and will not be their own loved ones returning. When they see fire come down from heaven, at the behest of some preacher, they will again believe that the miracle worker is a servant of the true God. All those shaped in the philosophy of science will be converted to unbiblical beliefs about the nature of man and the state of the dead when they shall see their departed loved ones appearing before them. They will be won over by the great apostate when they see these miracles. To those habituated in and living by the philosophy of science, seeing will be believing. "Many will be ensnared through the belief that spiritualism is a mere human imposture; when brought face to face with manifestations which they cannot but regard as supernatural, they will be deceived, and will be led to accept them as the great power of God." [16]

In view of these almost overpowering delusions, the question comes to you and to me: "Are the people of God now so firmly established upon His Word that they would not yield to the evidence of their senses? Would they, in such a crisis, cling to the Bible and the Bible only?" [17] The true followers of God in those trying hours must have a faith that is stronger than the witness of their senses. This trust in God's Word must be developed today.

Intellectual darkness during the Middle Ages was favorable to the success of the great apostasy. But "it will yet be demonstrated that a day of great intellectual light is equally *favorable for its* success. [18] In an age of faith it employed faith—or gullibility—for its successful advance. In an age of science it will use the method of science. The tools of the great apostate are fitted to the philosophy or convictions of the age.

"Antichrist is to perform his marvelous works in our sight. So closely will the counterfeit resemble the true that it will be impossible to distinguish between them except by the Holy Scriptures. By their testimony every statement and every miracle must be tested." [19]

In the gathering storm that will soon embroil us, we must follow the example of Jesus in His confrontation with Satan. "Jesus met Satan with the words of Scripture. 'It is written,' He said. In every temptation the weapon of His warfare was the Word of God. Satan demanded of Christ a miracle as a sign of His divinity. *But that which is greater than all miracles, a firm reliance upon a 'thus saith the Lord,' was a sign that could not be controverted.* So long as Christ held this position, the tempter could gain no advantage." [20] Miracles must never be a test of doctrine; rather, doctrine should be a test of miracles.

"Let us trust God's Word implicitly, remembering that we are His sons and daughters. Let us train ourselves to believe His Word. We hurt the heart of Christ by doubting, when He has given such evidence of His love." [21]

Although God is unlimited in both power and resources, He does not flaunt His power. He is therefore economical with miracles. As with all the different manifestations of the Spirit, they are used for the good of the church, not for purposes of exhibitionism. The manifestations are supplied in response to the particular need of the church at any particular time. Speaking of Paul's ministry at Ephesus, Ellen White says: "The apostles were not always able to work miracles at will. The Lord granted his servants this special power as the progress of his cause or the honor of his name required."[22]

This principle still holds good. God will grant the different manifestations of the Spirit as the needs of His church demand, since "to each is given the manifestation of the Spirit for the common good" (1 Cor. 12:7).

---

[1] See Ellen G. White, *Christ's Object Lessons*, p. 327.

[2] Ellen G. White, *Education*, p. 253.

[3] Ellen G. White, *Christ's Object Lessons*, p. 327.

[4] See Ellen G. White, *Testimonies*, vol. 8, pp. 187, 188.

[5] Ellen G. White, *The Ministry of Healing* (Mountain View, Calif.: Pacific Press Pub. Assn., 1905), p. 302.

[6] Frederick Dale Bruner, *A Theology of the Holy Spirit* (Grand Rapids, Mich.: William B. Eerdmans Publishing House, 1973), p. 296.

[7] Ellen G. White, *My Life Today*, p. 276.

[8] Ellen G. White, *The Desire of Ages*, p. 70.

[9] Ellen G. White, *The Ministry of Healing*, p. 502.

[10] Ellen G. White, *The Acts of the Apostles*, pp. 39, 40.

[11] William F. Arndt and F. Wilbur Gingrich in *A Greek English Lexicon of the New Testament* (University of Chicago Press, 1957), p. 29.

[12] Ellen G. White, *The Great Controversy* (Mountain View, Calif.: Pacific Press Pub. Assn., 1911), p. 612.

[13] Ellen G. White, *Selected Messages*, bk. 2, p. 51.

[14] *Ibid.*, p. 53.

[15] Ellen G. White, *The Great Controversy*, p. 588.

[16] *Ibid.*, p. 553.

[17] *Ibid.*, p. 625.

[18] *Ibid.*, pp. 572, 573.

[19] *Ibid.*, p. 593.

[20] Ellen G. White, *Review and Herald*, May 14, 1908.

[21] *Ibid.*, Feb. 28, 1907.

[22] Ellen G. White, *Sketches From the Life of Paul* (Washington, D.C.: Review and Herald Pub. Assn., 1974), p. 135.

CHAPTER 8

The Fruit of the Spirit

The very word "fruit" intrigues most of us.

While we were at Philippine Union College, we planted several papaya plants by our home. They grew rapidly, and after a few months most of the plants had reached a height of about 10 feet. How elated we were when the first blossoms appeared. This was a sure sign that our young plants would soon bear fruit.

God Himself is just as interested and enchanted with our fruit bearing as Christians. As we looked for fruit on our papaya trees, so He looks for fruit in our lives. "The fruit of the Spirit is love, joy, peace, patience, kindness, goodness, faithfulness, gentleness, self-control" (Gal. 5:22, 23).

"The paramount fruit of the Spirit is *love*. All that follow are but aspects of this divine quality. Just as various colors make up sunlight, so these graces together constitute love. Thus *joy* is love exulting; *peace* is love in repose; *long-suffering* is love untiring; *gentleness* is love enduring; *goodness* is love in action; *faith* is love in confidence; *meekness* is love under discipline; while *temperance* is love in self-control."[1]

The fruit of the Spirit will be manifest in the life of every genuine Christian. It is not the result of rules or discipline imposed from without, but is evidence of divine life within, just as fruit on a tree is evidence that the tree is alive. These graces are all found in Jesus. When He lives in us, they become ours.

A boy passed by a street corner where an electrician was working with the electric wires high up on an electric power pole. It was a warm, sunny summer day, but the electrician wore rubber boots. The boy looked at the man on the pole for a while. Then he asked, "Why do you wear those boots on such a hot day? Do you think we are going to get a downpour?"

The electrician replied, "Why no, sonny. I wear them to protect myself from an electric shock as I work with the wires. Electricity cannot go through rubber very well. And a strange thing with electricity is that if it cannot go through or out of a person, it does not get into him."

This is signally true of the love of God which is even a more potent power than electricity. The love of God can bring life, light, and power to a person only if it finds an outlet through him to others for the different manifestations of the fruit of the Spirit. The inflow of God's love depends on the outflow. The love of God in a Christian will therefore manifest itself in personal joy and peace; in long-suffering, gentleness, and goodness in his contact with others; and in faithfulness toward God and His will; in meekness among men; and temperance or self-control with reference to himself.

Years ago I owned some power tools. Among them was a jointer. A jointer is a machine which planes pieces of lumber. Before I purchased the jointer, I used to plane boards with a hand plane. It was tedious and hard work to plane many boards in that way, while with the jointer it took only a few seconds to plane or trim off half an inch of board. In order for me to benefit from my jointer, all that was necessary was to plug in, turn on the switch, and run my piece of lumber through the machine. Electric power furnished the jointer with power to perform its intended function. I myself could not possibly have produced sufficient power to operate it. But I did not need to worry about the power supply, so long as I was willing to plug in the cord and flip the electric switch.

The efficient work of the jointer connected with electric power illustrates our relationship to God and His power. We do not need to be worried about our lack of power. Our friend Jesus has all power (see Matt. 28:18, KJV). This power He is eager to place at our disposal as soon as we work in accordance with His plan. Our wisdom consists in finding out where God is going and then going with Him, for "as the will of man cooperates with the will of God, it becomes omnipotent."[2]

God is grievously disappointed when His professed followers fail to produce fruit. Their neglect to produce the fruit of the Spirit is not due to lack of power. God will abundantly supply this. Rather it is due to their unwilling attitude. God sorrows over their unwillingness, as Jesus grieved over Jerusalem that refused to accept His salvation (see Matt. 23:37). His final disposition of those who fail to fulfill His plan of fruit bearing is evident from Jesus' parable of the fruitless fig tree. It was cut down and cast into the fire to be burned, lest it cumber the ground (see Luke 13:6-9). But a true child in whom the Holy Spirit works as a transforming and empowering leaven cannot fail to produce fruit. This is his very nature, just as our papaya trees produced papayas. They just could not do anything else.

Fruit bearing is not an option; it is an ultimatum for every child of God. The fruit of the Spirit in our lives is visible evidence that we are becoming partakers of the divine nature and are being fitted for heavenly society. Thus all the nuances of the fruit of the Spirit will gradually appear in the experience of a Christian. This will show our fitness for heavenly society and our companionship with God and the unfallen angels.

While we lived in New England, a neighbor of ours thought spring with warm weather did not come soon enough. She thought her front-yard tree was too late in sprouting flowers and leaves. To make it appear that spring had come she tied artificial paper flowers on her tree. But although the paper flowers were beautiful and even brought joy and amusement to bypassers, these flowers did not produce fruit.

Neither does artificial Christianity produce the fruit of the Spirit. The person may outwardly look like a Christian, but if he has not been born again by the Spirit, he is dead despite all Christian veneer and appearance. The true graces of the Spirit will not appear in his life, since man himself cannot produce the fruit of the Spirit. Consequently, in order for the Spirit to appear in the life of a human mortal, He must be permitted to live within—to live out His life within the person who then will manifest the different facets of this divine fruit.

"Jesus 'has life in himself,' and this life He offers to impart freely, to souls that are dead in trespasses and sins. Yea, He shares with them His purity, His honor, and exaltation. . . . The sapless branch, ingrafted into the living vine, becomes a part of the vine. It lives while united to the vine. So the Christian lives by virtue of his union with Christ. The sinful and human is linked to the holy and divine. The believing soul abides in Christ, and becomes one with Him. When persons are closely united in the relations of this life, their tastes become similar, they come to love the same things. So those who abide in Christ will love the things which He loves. They will sacredly cherish and obey His commandments."[3]

By nature all of us have been dead in trespasses and sins. There are even dead members in the church of God. "The fact that men are in the church does not prove them Christians."[4] At times apparent fruit of the Spirit may have been "tied on" by laudable ethics of a humanistic society. To many an observer the fruitage of divine life within and the results of humanism are deceptively alike. A humanist may look like a Christian. Thus we may temporarily look like fruit-bearing Christians and still be dead in the sight of God. The flowers our neighbor tied on her tree were dead; they were not produced by the tree or part of it. Hence they produced no fruit.

Our papaya plants, mentioned earlier, produced papayas within less than a year after we set them out. They did not bear papayas to show they were papaya plants, however; they produced papayas because they were papaya plants. So it is with live, virile Christians. They produce the fruit of the Spirit not to show they are Christians; rather, they bear the fruit of the Spirit because they are Christians and the Spirit of God dwells within them.

Without a doubt all we as Christians would like to see the fruit of the Spirit in our lives. The fruit is the reproduction in us of the qualities of the personality of Christ. But this is only possible as we fully and completely surrender ourselves and our ways to the promptings of the Holy Spirit. He is willing to imbue us with true love—*agapē* love. This love is simply concern for our neighbor irrespective of whether he is attractive or not, irrespective of whether he is kind to us or not. Under all circumstances *agapē* love will do nothing but what is good for our neighbor. This is the mother love Luther told his students about in his *Table Talk.* "Mother love," he told them, "is stronger than the filth and scabbiness on a child, and so the love of God toward us is stronger than the dirt that clings to us."[5]

Goodness or virtue does not consist in doing nothing wrong. At the very best the refraining from doing evil is a mere negation. It is not virtue or goodness. A corpse in a coffin does not commit fornication, it does not swear, it does not lie, it does not steal. Is a corpse good because it does not do any of those bad acts? Is it fit for the kingdom of God? Emphatically, No.

To be good a person must first be alive. But it is not sufficient merely to be alive. To good he must do good (see Titus 3:8; 1 Peter 2:12). Only doing good reflects virtue. A person who does nothing wrong may be still just like a corpse. He does nothing. Such are not fit for fellowship with God and the angels, but are merely fit to be cast into the fire with the chaff and the tares.

The gospel prophet Isaiah in chapter 1:16 and 17 says, "Cease to do evil, learn to do good." That is a prescription for virtue. The saints admitted into the kingdom of God in the parable of Matthew 25 had done something positively and actively good. They had fed the hungry; they had given drink to the thirsty; they had befriended the stranger; the naked they had clothed; the sick they had visited; those imprisoned they had comforted. Those who do good while they are alive—and are virtuous, for such the kingdom of God is prepared (see Matt. 25:34). Those slated for damnation were not charged with having done anything bad, as we think of it. Sometimes we may have said in self-justification, "What wrong did I do?" That question may clear us before an earthly accuser, but it will not vindicate you and me when we appear before the King of the universe at the last assize.

The fruit of the Spirit is a direct result of and must needs spring from a union with Jesus through the Spirit, for Jesus said, "Apart from me you can do nothing" (John 15:5).

F. E. Marsh relates the following experience: "I picked up a small notebook one day, and as I opened it a delightful fragrance of violets greeted me. I could not think at the moment how the book could smell so sweet, then I remembered a friend had given me some violets at Santa Barbara, on the Pacific Coast, and I had pressed some of them between the leaves on a journey of 7,000 miles to England. . . . Thus the things which the violets touched were made like themselves, sweet.[6]

In this way the Spirit imparts His character to those who are permeated by His holiness and sweetened by His grace.

The fruit of the Spirit is in full harmony with the law of God. After enumerating all the different aspects the apostle concludes: "There is no law against such things as these" (Gal. 5:23, TEV). The Christians bearing the fruit of the Spirit or manifesting these fruits of character are indeed fulfilling the law, for "love is the fulfilling of the law" (Rom. 13:10).

---

[1] *Questions on Doctrine* (Washington, D.C.: Review and Herald Pub. Assn., 1957), p. 115.

[2] Ellen G. White, *Christ's Object Lessons*, p. 333.

[3] Ellen G. White, *Our High Calling* (Washington, D.C.: Review and Herald Pub. Assn., 1961), p. 145.

[4] Ellen G. White, *Christ's Object Lessons*, p. 74.

[5] *Luther's Works* (Philadelphia: Fortress Press, 1967), vol. 54, p. 70.

[6] F. E. Marsh, *Emblems of the Holy Spirit,* pp. 71, 72.

CHAPTER 9

The Guidance of the Spirit

Jesus arouses the sinner from sleep in spiritual death and plants within the repentant person eternal life and "places him under the guidance of the Holy Spirit."[1]

Jesus said to the disciples, "The Counselor, the Holy Spirit, whom the Father will send in my name, he will teach you all things, and bring to your remembrance all that I have said to you" (John 14:26). The Spirit was both to remind them of what Jesus had taught and to teach them what they would need to know in the future, as well as guide them amid all the vexing problems of life.

As an ambassador speaks in the name of his home government to a foreign government, so the Spirit speaks to men in the name of Jesus, or in His behalf, and with His authority. In this way Jesus perpetuated His earthly teaching ministry through the Spirit. "The Lord acts through the Holy Spirit; for it is His representative."[2]

The Spirit is a living, personal teacher. He is the needed illuminator of the Word of God. Only through His help can we rightly understand the Word of truth. Many of us at some time or another have listened to a great teacher and then we have said to ourselves, "If I could only have such a teacher, then I'm sure I could learn." But in the Spirit all of us may have a superbly competent and peerless teacher. "God can teach you more in one moment by His Holy Spirit than you could learn from the great men of the earth."[3]

But to profit from the Spirit's help, we must be teachable. Even a superior teacher can never help a student unless the student himself realizes that he needs help—or until he becomes teachable. The same is true in our relationship with the Holy Spirit. Unless we are willing to receive His help, He can do nothing for us. We must come to the place where we choose not to follow our own impulses and cherished notions, but rather follow the biddings of the Holy Spirit to us through the Word. The true follower of Jesus will do nothing without seeking the constant advice and guidance of God's Word and the Holy Spirit. "Lord, what do you want me to do?" is the Christian's continual attitude and question. This was the question that Paul asked the Lord on the Damascus road (see Acts 22:10).

The teachableness of a Christian is indicated by his refusal to remain in the realm of mere belief or intellectual faith; his faith will be experimental rather than theoretical. Under the guidance of the Spirit, the heavenly mind of thought and belief will transform the earthly patterns of behavior and action. This is genuine saving faith which "works through love" (Gal. 5:6, TEV).

Profession does not make us children of God. Paul identifies God's true children by saying, "All who are led by the Spirit of God are the sons of God" (Rom. 8:14). By following God's directions and doing His will, we may be more closely related to Jesus than even His mother, sisters, and brothers (see Matt. 12:50). Ellen White points up who rules those who are not led by the Spirit. "Every man, woman, and child that is not under the control of the Spirit of God is under the influence of Satan's sorcery."[4]

But mere obedience to God's will, as good and commendable as it may be, will not make us fit for heavenly society. "Love to God is the very foundation of religion. To engage in His service merely from hope of reward or fear of punishment would avail nothing."[5] Those who finally are to live with God in heaven will be characterized on earth by willing obedience to His will. The prophet says, "If you are willing and obedient, you shall eat the good of the land" (Isa. 1:19). Further, it is not those who merely believe in Christ's imminent return that are going to meet Him in peace and live with Him in glory throughout eternity, but "all who have loved his appearing" (2 Tim. 4:8).

When we think back on our childhood days, most of us recall that at times we obeyed our parents unwillingly. Our parents knew the difference between willing and unwilling obedience. In the same way God discerns the difference between willing and unwilling obedience.

Willing obedience does not always spring spontaneously even from the heart of a child of God. As children and youth we had to educate ourselves to obey our parents willingly and readily. In the same way we as Christians choose to educate ourselves so that we come to the place where we obey God willingly and readily.

I can recall several occasions when I knew God's will, but I did not like to comply with it. I did not try to delude myself by telling myself that I liked God's will when I definitely did not. Rather, I frankly confessed to God that I knew His will, but that I did not like it. Then I told Him, "God, I cannot change my heart or my attitude, but You can do it. You have promised, 'A new heart I will give you, and a new spirit I will put within you; and I will take out of your flesh the heart of stone and give you a heart of flesh. And I will put my spirit within you' (Eze. 36:26, 27). Please, God, fulfill that promise so that I may come to the place where I like to do Your will."

This promise God has fulfilled for me several times, and He will do it for us all, provided we are willing. "You are not able, of yourself, to bring your purposes and desires and inclinations into submission to the will of God; but if you are 'willing to be made willing,' God will accomplish the work for you, even 'casting down imaginations, and every high thing that exalteth itself against the knowledge of God, bringing into captivity every thought to the obedience of Christ' 2 Corinthians 10:5."[6]

From the willing follower of Jesus nothing is withheld. God delights to help him. James assures us of His help. He writes, "If any of you lacks wisdom, let him ask God who gives to all men generously and without reproaching, and it will be given him" (James 1:5). The psalmist gives the same assurance: "He leads the humble in what is right, and teaches the humble his way" (Ps. 25:9); "Who is the man that fears the Lord? Him will he instruct in the way that he should choose" (Ps. 25:12); "I will instruct you and teach you the way you should go; I will counsel you with my eye upon you" (Ps. 32:8). And the gospel prophet Isaiah verifies God's promise of intimate guidance of the Spirit by saying: "Your ears shall hear a word behind you, saying, 'This is the way, walk in it,' when you turn to the right or when you turn to the left" (Isa. 30:21).

The average person glories in being directed from within, or being self-directed, making his own choices and decisions, rather than being told by some other person what to do. But the Christian is not satisfied by being inner-directed or going solely by his mind or reason; rather he chooses to be guided by God's Word through the Holy Spirit.

When Moses thought he was ready to lead his kinsmen out of Egypt, he followed his own mind and murdered an Egyptian. He thought that this action would indicate to the enslaved Israelites that he was prepared to be their deliverer (see Ex. 2:11, 12). But God did not at the time deem Moses prepared for the emancipator's role; his inclination to rely on his own judgment and reason disqualified him. His self-sufficiency must have been firmly established in his mind, since 40 years of sheepherding in Midian was required to disabuse him of his self-trust and teach him dependence on God. But during these 40 years Moses learned to depend on God and follow His directions.

When he stood before the foam-capped waves of the Red Sea at the head of the departing Israelites, he did not follow his own notions concerning how to extricate his people from destruction before the advancing Egyptians. He asked God what to do; and God, contrary to all human wisdom, told him, "Tell the people to go forward" (Ex. 14:15). When the Israelites later were troubled with bitter water in the desert, Moses again asked God what to do; and again God led him (see Ex. 15:25). God did not expect Moses to solve his problems single-handedly; He wanted him to come to Him for help.

As the leader of Israel, Moses was the executor of God's will and plans. He was not to devise the plans and policies for Israel. It was his privilege and also his responsibility to go to God and ask Him for guidance in any and every case of perplexity. Thus Moses learned to rely on divine wisdom. When on one occasion he did not know what to do with an Israelite who had cursed God, he placed him in detention until God would instruct him (see Lev. 24:10-12). In due time God told him what to do.

When the leaders of Israel in the days of Joshua tried to act responsibly and neglected to ask God for guidance with reference to the Gibeonite request for an alliance, they made the wrong decision. The result of this neglect to consult God precipitated an immediate crisis for Israel (see Joshua 9).

To a proud mind it is not pleasing to be dependent or to ask for counsel and help. The proud individual would rather stand alone and rely on his own resources, though paltry they be. Selfishly he reasons: "I'll handle it myself; I'll manage, without any help or advice from you, God. You mind Your own business of running the universe; I'll take care of my own problems by using the intelligence and reasoning ability You have given me." It is humiliating for him to request help. But it is man's spurning of God's love that separates man from God and makes it ultimately impossible for a person to ask God for help. The selfish person draws apart and feels compelled to solve all his problems alone.

As God's children, we know that He loves us, and we love Him. Bound to our heavenly Father by love, we feel free and are glad to come to Him who is willing and eager to share His wisdom with His earth children.

It is God's plan that His children constantly sustain an intimate and close relationship to Him so that they may at all times and under all circumstances ask and receive help and guidance from Him. At times this relationship is im-

paired. But how we cherish the memory of occasions of intimate and immediate communion with God! We experience joy and satisfaction and thank
God for His nearness and guidance. We remember these occasions as times
when God enabled us to speak the right words and do the proper deeds, even
in perplexing situations, because we were guided by His Spirit.

To some, such an anticipated close relationship to God is mystical and
unreasonable. But a spiritually scintillating Christian experience is mystical
and will forever remain irrational to the person who does not personally
and intimately know God as his Friend.

Simeon enjoyed an intimate relationship with God. Thus the Spirit
told him to go to the temple on the day the child Jesus was being dedicated to God. From among the several boys who were being dedicated to
God that day, he chose Jesus. The officiating priest did not recognize Jesus
as the coming Messiah, since He was oblivious to the promptings of the
Holy Spirit. But Simeon recognized Him because God mystically and personally told him which babe was the Messiah. Some of the other boys
whom Simeon bypassed might also have been born in Bethlehem as the
firstborn child to mothers who were of the tribe of Judah, as had been
foretold by the prophets (see Micah 5:2; Isa. 7:14; Gen. 4:9, 10; Dan. 9:24-
27). But only Simeon's intimate communion with God and his response
to the promptings of the Holy Spirit enabled him to single out Jesus and
acclaim Him as the Promised One on that particular day, in accordance
with the writings of the prophets (see Luke 2:25-35).

The only safe course for a child of God is to have the Spirit constantly
living within as a heavenly guide. Apart from this the domination of the
carnal nature will reassert itself and thrust the child of God back into sin.
Really, "We are not safe for a moment unless guided and controlled by the
Holy Spirit."[7] If we persistently refuse this divine guidance, we will be
guided by emissaries from the prince of darkness, since "messengers from
the prince of darkness attend all who refuse to be controlled by the Holy
Spirit."[8] We as children of God should be as susceptible to the Holy
Spirit's prompting as was Mary when she anointed the feet of Jesus at
Simon's Feast. When her accusers asked her why she had wasted "three
hundred pence" worth (see John 12:3-5) on Jesus, she had no answer; she
could give no reason for her action. "The Holy Spirit had planned for her,
and she had obeyed His promptings."[9] An unseen presence had spoken to
her mind and soul and moved her to her kind deed for Jesus.

After preaching a sermon entitled "The Good Shepherd," during his
second evangelistic series at Edinburgh in 1874, Dwight L. Moody asked

his singing evangelist, Ira David Sankey, to sing something appropriate. Sankey immediately thought of the Shepherd Psalm, but realized that it was not suitable for a solo. Suddenly he heard a voice whisper to him, "Sing the hymn you found on the train."

Shortly before this on a train ride from Glasgow to Edinburgh, Sankey had found in the *Christian Age* a poem by Elizabeth Cecilia Douglass Clephane, "There Were Ninety and Nine." With a silent prayer for divine help he placed the newspaper clipping with the words on the piano and began playing and singing, composing the tune as he sang. Sankey was submissive to and guided by the Holy Spirit as he composed the tune for the lyric "There Were Ninety and Nine."

As we approach the end-time, it will become even more imperatively important that we enjoy this intimate guidance of God through the Spirit. "Falsehood will be so mingled with truth, that only those who have the guidance of the Holy Spirit will be able to distinguish truth from error."[10] Today is our opportunity to cultivate this intimacy with God through the Spirit.

Physicians give prescriptions and expect their patients to use the medicine prescribed. If your physician asks you as a patient to take a certain medicine for two weeks, he is not happy if you take it for only three days. God too gives you and me prescriptions. How well do you and I follow His prescriptions?

"Our great Physician requires of every soul unquestioning submission. We are never to prescribe for our own care. Christ must have the entire management of will and action. . . . Genuine faith is followed by love, and love by obedience. All the powers and passions of the converted man are brought under the control of Christ. His Spirit is a renewing power, transforming to the divine image all who receive it."[11]

The cost of such an intimate fellowship with the Creator is renunciation of our independence and a willing and glad-hearted acceptance of the total and constantly unveiled will of God.

God's wisdom and guidance are available to His children even in split-moment decisions. Nehemiah, the king's cupbearer, in standing before King Artaxerxes, sent a petition to his heavenly Father for wisdom to speak the right words in answer to the king's invitation that he present his request. Instantly God granted his request and gave him the words to speak to the king so that the monarch's sympathy was elicited, rather than his prejudice aroused (see Neh. 2:1-4). To pray as Nehemiah prayed in his hour of need is a resource at the command of every Christian. Toilers in the busy walks of life, crowded and almost overwhelmed with perplexity, can always send their petitions to God for divine guidance.

Jesus knew that the experience of His loyal witnesses would not always be calm and peaceful. Persecution would be theirs. But in spite of this they were not to be intimidated and fearful of what to say.

When persecution began and the deacon Stephen was questioned about his faith, his opponents "could not withstand the wisdom and the Spirit with which he spoke" (Acts 6:10). To him was the promise of Jesus fulfilled. "When they deliver you up, do not be anxious how you are to speak or what you are to say; for what you are to say will be given you in that hour; for it is not you who speak, but the Spirit of your Father speaking through you" (Matt. 10:19, 20).

God will have loyal witnesses now and in the future as He has had in the past. At his trial before the imperial authorities the apostle Paul was conscious of divine help after all human friends had forsaken him. In his letter to Timothy he says: "At my first defense no one took my part; all deserted me. May it not be charged against them! But the Lord stood by me and gave me strength to proclaim the message fully, that all the Gentiles might hear it. So I was rescued from the lion's mouth" (2 Tim. 4:16, 17).

Describing Paul's appearance before Nero, Ellen White characterizes him as "the advocate of truth." She says further: "Faithful among the faithless, loyal among the disloyal, he stands as God's representative, and his voice is as a voice from heaven. There is no fear, no sadness, no discouragement, in word or look. . . . His words are as a shout of victory above the roar of battle." [12]

In like manner the Spirit's guidance will be ours in moments of harassment for His sake. We should not be fearful even though there may be unjust suffering for us in the future. The apostolic Christians thanked God for the honor of being considered "worthy to suffer disgrace for the sake of Jesus" (Acts 5:41). We should not expect to possess the courage of martyrs for today. It is true of courage as of daily bread. It is only granted when needed. As we are faithful today our courage and words will not fail us in some dire moment in the future need. Not even the disciples were granted the fortitude of martyrs until their moment of need. "The disciples were not endowed with the courage and fortitude of the martyrs until such grace was needed. Then the Savior's promise [of Matt. 10:19] was fulfilled." [13]

As we today follow the guidance of God through His Spirit, He will always be our sufficiency in any time of need. "My God will supply every need of yours according to his riches in glory in Christ Jesus" (Phil. 4:19).

[1] Ellen G. White, *Selected Messages,* bk. 1, p. 349.

[2] Ellen G. White, *Sons and Daughters of God* (Washington, D.C.: Review and Herald Pub. Assn., 1955), p. 282.

[3] Ellen G. White, *Testimonies to Ministers,* p. 119.

[4] Ellen G. White, *Messages to Young People* (Nashville, Tenn.: Southern Pub. Assn., 1930), p. 278.

[5] Ellen G. White, *Patriarchs and Prophets,* p. 523.

[6] Ellen G. White, *Thoughts From the Mount of Blessing,* p. 142.

[7] Ellen G. White, *Our High Calling,* p. 187.

[8] Ellen G. White, *The Desire of Ages,* p. 656.

[9] *Ibid.,* p. 560.

[10] Ellen G. White, manuscript 43, 1893.

[11] Ellen G. White, *Testimonies,* vol. 5, p. 219.

[12] Ellen G. White, *My Life Today,* p. 65.

[13] Ellen G. White, *The Desire of Ages,* p. 354.

CHAPTER 10

Life Through the Spirit

I t is the Spirit that gives life, the flesh is of no avail" (John 6:63). Through Spirit baptism divine life was planted within us.

There is no new life in us apart from the Spirit. The Spirit is God. As such He is life. And it is only through the Spirit that life is imparted to us—both physical and spiritual. "The impartation of the Spirit is the impartation of the life of Christ." [1]

The Spirit alone can make Jesus' saving works for us effective unto salvation. We may speak eloquently and movingly of Jesus and His incarnation, suffering, death, resurrection, ascension, and even His intercession for us today at the right hand of God. But not one or even all these vital ministries of Jesus will bring us salvation. Satan rejoices as long as we limit our presentation to these aspects of the story of redemption. "The Spirit was to be given as a regenerating agent, and without this the sacrifice of Christ would have been of no avail." [2]

In the visit of Jesus with Nicodemus, the following conversation developed: " 'Truly, truly, I say to you, unless one is born anew, he cannot see the kingdom of God.' Nicodemus said to him, 'How can a man be born when he is old? Can he enter a second time into his mother's womb and be born?' Jesus answered, 'Truly, truly I say to you, unless one is born of water and the Spirit, he cannot enter the kingdom of God. That which is born of the flesh is flesh, and that which is born of the Spirit is spirit' " (John 3:3-6).

Born again in John 3 actually means "born from above." Regeneration is therefore not our natural life brought up to the highest level of attainment, but rather divine life imparted from above to us who were previously dead in trespasses and sin (see Eph. 2:1).

Nicodemus had come to Jesus aiming to enter into a theoretical discussion about truth. "But Jesus laid bare the foundation principles of truth. He said to Nicodemus, It is not theoretical knowledge you need so much as spiritual regeneration. You need not to have your curiosity satisfied, but to have a new heart. You must receive a new life from above before you can appreciate heavenly things."[3]

The new birth is a regeneration and a partaking of the divine nature. As the Holy Spirit applies the precious promises of the Word of God to our minds and hearts, we become partakers of the divine nature (see 2 Peter 1:4). Indeed, "in Christ, man is privileged to become a partaker of the divine nature."[4]

The apostle Paul in his letter to Titus also emphasizes the necessity of "regeneration and renewal in the Holy Spirit" (Titus 3:5). Paul also makes it clear that "if any one is in Christ, he is a new creation; the old has passed away, behold, the new has come" (2 Cor. 5:17). Paul says further, "You are not in the flesh, you are in the Spirit, if in fact the Spirit of God dwells in you" (Rom. 8:9).

Through Jesus and the Spirit mortal men possess eternal life. "This is the testimony, that God gave us eternal life, and this life is in his Son. He who has the Son has life; he who has not the Son of God has not life" (1 John 5:11, 12). The Holy Spirit is power and works as a living, active agent through the new life created in the soul. Today you and I as born-again Christians have eternal life.

The presence of the Spirit in our lives is God's reminder that eternal life is ours now. "If Christ be in you, the body is dead because of sin; but the Spirit is life because of righteousness" (Rom. 8:10). "Those who seek Christ in His true character have within them the divine nature, having escaped the corruptions that are in the world through lust."[5]

The only way Christ can live in man is through His Spirit. Jesus interjects Himself by His Spirit into your life and mine and into human affairs. "The Holy Spirit is to be in us a divine indweller,"[6] and God works in and through us by His Spirit.

The Spirit mediates this new life through the word. Jesus said: "The words that I have spoken to you are spirit and life" (John 6:63). As the divine life within began through the word, so the Spirit purposes that the new life within be sustained by the word. Peter says, "As newborn babes, desire the sincere milk of the word, that ye may grow thereby" (1 Peter 2:2, KJV).

No life can be sustained without food. This is true of both animal and vegetable life. We eat regularly and daily to keep physically strong and healthy. Neither can we sustain our spiritual life without nourishment. Nor are we spiritual camels so that we can survive spiritually by eating only once in a while. Further, to live physically we must breathe. Physical life will ebb out in less than five minutes if we stop breathing. Since "the Holy Spirit is the breath of spiritual life in the soul,"[7] without Him our spiritual life will cease. To live spiritually we must of necessity have the breath of the Spirit and eat Spirit-produced food by reading and studying the Word.

The Bible was given through the Spirit. It was "inspired by God" (2 Tim. 3:16)—literally "God-breathed"[8]—as the spokesmen for God "were borne along by the Spirit as a ship is borne along by the wind."[9] Its vital power is due to its divine origin. The Word is the medium used by the Spirit to bring to us life from above and to sustain it within us.

When a baby is born, the parents hope that it will grow. Hence they feed it according to the pediatrician's instructions and weigh it regularly to see how much it is gaining from week to week. As parents hope their child might grow and develop, so God hopes you and I as Christians might grow. The apostle says, "Grow in grace and knowledge of our Lord and Savior Jesus Christ" (2 Peter 3:18).

But even though a person has been born again and has become a partaker of the divine nature, no changes may in some instances become immediately visible. Jesus used leaven as an illustration of divine life within and of the transforming power of the grace of God through the Holy Spirit in a believer's life (see Matt. 13:33). The leaven is placed in the dough. At first no change is noticed in the dough, but little by little it begins to work. Ultimately the nature of the whole lump of dough will be changed. This transformation God desires to effect in every believer—in you and me—through the implantation of His Spirit.

But this change is often accompanied by conflict. The average person who has been born again and has new life within at times experiences turmoil. Conflict rages between the old carnal self and its desires and the promptings of the new spiritual life.

The apostle Paul in Galatians 4 presents this conflict within the newly converted person in a parable from Abraham's household after the birth of Isaac. For several years after the birth of Ishmael as the heir apparent, and before the birth of Isaac, peace and happiness reigned in Abraham's home. With the birth of Isaac, however, conflict began. With the years this conflict became intolerable. Finally God called Abraham and told him that he must cast out Ishmael from his house (see Gen. 21:10-12). Cast out the idol of his heart? This was difficult for Abraham, but finally he realized it was better to shed a few tears at Ishmael's departure than to have conflict in his home. And so Ishmael went.

Paul tells us that the two sons of Abraham are symbolic of the two natures within man after he has become a son of God through His promise. "Now we, brethren, like Isaac, are children of promise. But as at that time he who was born according to the flesh persecuted him who was born according to the Spirit, so it is now. But what does the scripture say? 'Cast out the slave and her son; for the son of the slave shall not inherit with the son of the free woman.' So, brethren, we are not children of the slave but of the free woman" (Gal. 4:28-31).

It is not pleasant to have two pugilists within. Abraham knew it; you and I have experienced it.

We should remember that the carnal nature is not easily dislodged or ousted; it claims squatter's rights within us. It was there first, just as was Ishmael. "It may take time to attain perfect submission to God's will, but we can never stop short of it and be fitted for Heaven." [10]

In 2 Corinthians 3:18 Paul says, "We all, . . . beholding the glory of the Lord, are being changed into his likeness from one degree of glory to another." This shows that our conformation to the image of our Lord is produced gradually. It is a progressive experience that began at regeneration and continues through our sanctification. But "if the eye is fixed on Christ, the work of the Spirit ceases not until the soul is conformed to His image." [11]

We who were once dead in sin (see Eph. 2:1, KJV) to the wishes of God are, as Christ's followers, to become "dead to sin" (Rom. 6:11). Through baptism we identified ourselves with Jesus in His death on the cross. We died with Him, and as Christians our "life is hid with Christ in God" (Col. 3:3).

But the old life of sin is urging its continued supremacy, just as Ishmael was. However, "if by the Spirit you put to death the deeds of the body you will live" (Rom. 8:13) eternally. The Greek tense makes it plain that to "put to death the deeds of the body" is a continuous attitude on the believer's part. Constant warfare rages between the Spirit and the flesh, as between Ishmael and Isaac. But Paul affirms that "if you are guided by the Spirit you will not fulfill the desires of your lower nature. That nature sets its desires against the Spirit, while the Spirit fights against it" (Gal. 5:16, 17, NEB).

"The outlook of the lower nature is enmity with God; it is not subject to the law of God; indeed it cannot be: those who live on such a level cannot possibly please God" (Rom. 8:7, 8, NEB). "Make no mistake about this: God is not to be fooled; a man reaps what he sows. If he sows seed in the field of his lower nature, he will reap from it a harvest of corruption, but if he sows in the field of the Spirit, the Spirit will bring him a harvest of eternal life" (Gal. 6:7, 8, NEB). Living according to the flesh or one's lower nature is ruinous. As Paul says, "I know that nothing good lodges in me—in my unspiritual nature" (Rom. 7:18, NEB). Consequently, as followers of Jesus we "put no confidence in the flesh" (Phil. 3:3).

As did Jesus, we choose to subordinate the demands of our human nature to the biddings of the Spirit. "In Christ there was a subjection of the human to the divine. He clothed his divinity with humanity, and placed his own person under obedience to divinity."[12]

Paul therefore bids us to "not gratify the desires of the flesh," but to "walk by the Spirit" (Gal. 5:16). As followers of Jesus, we purpose to live "no longer by the dictates of our sinful nature, but in obedience to the promptings of the Spirit" (Rom. 8:4, Phillips).

In some cases growth is seen for only a short time after conversion, and then it becomes obvious that there is no longer any life. In seeing this, some are prone to say that a person with such an experience was never converted. But that need not be true.

As a family we have enjoyed planting gardens. After cultivating the soil, we planted seeds. Soon we saw our carrots and beets come up. The little plants were indeed alive and growing. But even though they grew initially, it did not follow that they would continue to grow. Sometimes a garden that was well cared for, and where all the vegetables came up and grew well for a while, soon becomes neglected. The small, spindly tender carrots cannot cope successfully with the weeds, but are choked to death.

As some of the small vegetables in our garden had to be cared for after they started growing, so the new life in the Spirit must also be cultivated. The weeds that would choke it must be removed.

Many years ago when I first came to a Christian school and gave my life to God, a schoolmate noticed some of these weeds in my mind. Some of these weeds were songs lingering in my mind that reminded of and led to sin; another weed was the books I had read before giving my heart to God; still another weed was sinful thought to which my mind was habituated. Knowing this, my friend wrote out several Bible texts on a slip of paper and gave them to me. She said, "Memorize these texts; and when some of the old sinful thoughts come back to you, then recite some of these texts. You can't at all times recite them aloud, but repeat them silently in your mind. Memorize also some of the hymns from the hymnbook; and when the old songs come back to you, hum or sing one of these hymns in your heart."

As a young man I followed this advice. In this way a change was brought into my thinking pattern. I continued this practice until I had committed hundreds of texts to memory. On innumerable occasions I have repeated some of these words of promise from God and turned back the tempter. The thorns must be removed from the converted mind in order to enable the good seed to grow and produce the fruit of salvation. "If the heart is not kept under the control of God, if the Holy Spirit does not work unceasingly to refine and enable the character, the old habits will reveal themselves in life." [13]

Nothing was wrong with the seed first planted in the soul. Nor can it be said that new life had not arisen within. The Spirit had effected a regeneration. Divine life was sprouting within. But, alas, even divine life may be choked. We should always remember that it is possible to begin in the Spirit and still end up in the flesh. Abraham followed God's advice and drove Ishmael from his house, even though it was a painful experience. Isaac, the son of promise or the new nature, was to hold sway. As Christians, we too will follow Abraham's example and grow in grace, by saying resolutely No to what we know is contrary to God's will. Like Abraham you and I will tell "our Ishmael" to get out of our soul temple.

[1] Ellen G. White, *Gospel Workers*, p. 285.
[2] Ellen G. White, *The Desire of Ages*, p. 671.
[3] *Ibid.*, p. 171.
[4] Ellen G. White, *Review and Herald*, November 29, 1898.
[5] Ellen G. White, *Selected Messages*, bk. 1, p. 137.
[6] Ellen G. White, *Review and Herald*, June 29, 1897.
[7] Ellen G. White, *The Desire of Ages*, p. 805.
[8] Francis D. Nichol, *Seventh-day Adventist Bible Commentary*, vol. 7, p. 344.
[9] *Ibid.*, p. 602.
[10] Ellen G. White, *Testimonies*, vol. 3, p. 538.
[11] Ellen G. White, *The Desire of Ages*, p. 302.
[12] Ellen G. White, *Review and Herald*, Nov. 9, 1897.
[13] Ellen G. White, *Christ's Object Lessons*, p. 50.

CHAPTER 11

The Restorer of the Image of God in Man

G od created Adam in His own image. Thus formed, Adam was perfect in his innocence. Perfect, but not with all his faculties fully developed.

But even in his newly created perfection Adam was not a replica of God. In a way he was like God, as a baby resembles its father and mother, for Adam "bore, in his physical, mental, and spiritual nature, a likeness to His Maker."[1] As God looked upon His completed creation with its climax in Adam and Eve, He saw that "it was very good" (Gen. 1:31).

God probably has many other worlds throughout His immense universe peopled with happy, peaceful, intelligent beings. But Adam and Eve "were a new and distinct order."[2] Man was, in some respects, like God Himself, and God looked forward to many happy moments of fellowship with Adam and Eve and their descendants, just as married couples look forward with joy to future fellowship with their children.

"God is love" (1 John 4:8). "Infinite love—how great it is! God made the world to enlarge heaven. He desires a larger family of created intelligences."[3] As a child in a family according to God's plan is to be the result of love between husband and wife, so man came into existence because of God's love. Parents who already have several children sometimes adopt another child. They like another person to share and enjoy their happiness of physical, mental, and spiritual well-being.

God wanted to enlarge his family; He wanted more free-willed intelligences to share His joy. Thus He created Adam and Eve and endowed them with procreative powers so that the whole earth might ultimately be populated. Adam and Eve and their posterity were to be cocreators with the Creator in peopling this earth. In this way they were different from the angels. The angels do not procreate, for they neither marry nor are given in marriage (see Matt. 22:30). To man was given the distinct privilege of helping God to populate the earth (see Gen. 1:28).

Heaven shared God's joy and satisfaction in the creation of this earth and man. "The morning stars sang together, and all the sons of God shouted for joy" (Job 38:7). Heaven's inhabitants "took a deep and joyful interest in the creation of the world and of man."[4]

Although perfect, as babies are perfect, Adam and Eve were not statically to remain at the level on which they were created. It was God's purpose that they should grow and develop and pass from innocence to virtue. "The longer man lived the more fully he should reveal this [God's] image—the more fully reflect the glory of the Creator. All his faculties were capable of development; their capacity and vigor were continually to increase."[5] A glorious future beckoned Adam and Eve.

For their inner mentor and continuous guide in growth and development, God gave Adam and Eve the constant companionship of the Third Person of the Godhead as their indwelling guest.[6]

But Lucifer, the fallen cherub who had been ousted from heaven before the creation of Adam and Eve,[7] purposed otherwise. "As soon as the Lord through Jesus Christ created our world, and placed Adam and Eve in the garden of Eden, Satan announced his purpose to conform to his own nature the father and mother of all humanity, and to unite them with his own ranks of rebellion. He was determined to efface the image of God from the human posterity, and to trace his own image upon the soul in place of the divine image."[8]

One day when Eve had strayed from the side of Adam and found herself at the tree of knowledge, the serpent began to speak to her. The serpent did not then crawl on its belly as it now does; rather, it was the most dazzlingly beautiful and most intelligent of all the animals in the garden. Eve was astonished that it could talk (it was not the serpent who spoke, but Lucifer the fallen angel who was using it as a medium). By parleying with him Eve was seduced and trapped into going contrary to God's will.

When Adam learned what Eve had done, he deliberately chose to ignore God's advice and ate of the forbidden fruit to share her fate. Eve was tricked into sin; Adam chose to sin (see 1 Tim. 2:14).

By eating of the forbidden fruit the Edenic couple relinquished their loyalty to God. As a result, their natures became changed. Prior to their eating of the forbidden fruit they had been in harmony with God; but "when man transgressed the divine law, his nature became evil, and he was in harmony, and not at variance, with Satan."[9]

Through sin or disloyalty to God, Adam's status in relation to creation also changed. Originally he had dominion over the earth (see Gen. 1:26). But by obeying Satan, Adam virtually handed over his rulership to the enemy, and he became Satan's servant (see Rom. 6:16). Neither was Adam, the son of God (see Luke 3:38), any longer to represent this earth among the other sons of God in the heavenly council. From now on Satan appeared as the representative from this earth (see Job 1:6, 7).

God's original plan of deriving pleasure from Adam and Eve and their descendants' companionship Satan thus frustrated. Their choice to obey Satan rather than Him, and reflect his image rather than God's, filled His heart with sorrow.

But God's plans know no permanent defeat; His plan for the earth will ultimately be fulfilled. It will even be fulfilled on time, since "God's purposes know no haste and no delay."[10]

Even though the human race has been nearly ruined in the fires kindled by sin, God purposes to bring forth from this holocaust men and women who are to excel even the angels in moral excellence. "For God so loved the world that he gave his only Son, that whoever believes in him should not perish but have eternal life" (John 3:16).

We rejoice that Jesus is willing and able to save us by His grace when we helplessly come to Him in repentance for our sins. He freely justifies us and accounts us righteous, as though we had never sinned.

Young people are commonly advised not to marry anyone in order to change the character of the spouse. That may be human. But God's plan is diametrically different. He marries all who come to Him through the forensic declaration of justification by faith. Then He seals them with His Spirit, as a constant reminder that they belong to Him, and through the power of the Spirit, He sets about to change them.

He has no intention of leaving us in the state in which we come to Him. His sole purpose is to change us. Justification is indeed our title to heaven and will always remain the foundation of our hope of salvation. But to fit us for heavenly society He plans to free us from sin, or sanctify us, or make us holy. As the foundation for a house is not built to be an end in itself, so justification is not the end of God's plan for us. If a wife's impregnation by her husband does not produce any change in her life, everyone knows that she is not pregnant. Likewise, if no change occurs in the life, no justification has been effected. God's purpose in justification is to change us, as the sole purpose of a foundation is the construction of a house. God justifies us in order to restore in us His own image of holiness.

All who accept His plan of salvation He plans to restore "to the image of his Son" (Rom. 8:29). Even though we are bruised by sin, God plans that each person who chooses shall become a new person. "Therefore, if any one is in Christ, he is a new creation; the old has passed away, behold, the new has come" (2 Cor. 5:17). God plans to recreate everyone who is willing.

God has delegated the Spirit to accomplish this work in repentant sinners, just as He assigned the Son to pay the price for our redemption. We are "chosen and destined by God the Father and sanctified by the Spirit for obedience to Jesus Christ and for sprinkling with his blood" (1 Peter 1:2). "Because God chose you from the beginning to be saved, through sanctification by the Spirit and belief in the truth" (2 Thess. 2:13).

"It is the Holy Spirit, the Comforter, which Jesus said He would send into the world, that changes our character into the image of Christ; and when this is accomplished, we reflect, as in a mirror, the glory of the Lord." [11]

After the Spirit has occupied our soul temple, He sets about to deliver us from slavery to sin. He guarantees that he who believes shall be saved. "For sin will have no dominion over you" (Rom. 6:14). The only salvation that exists is salvation from sin; there is no salvation except from sin.

Jesus hates sin; He hates it with an intense hatred because He knows that unless His people will be cleansed from it it will destroy them. His very name guarantees that He will free every willing follower from its destructive power. The angel said to Joseph when he announced Mary's firstborn son's birth, "She will bear a son, and you shall call his name Jesus, for he will save his people from their sins" (Matt. 1:21).

The prophet Isaiah repeatedly stresses the flammability of sin. "The strong shall become tow, and his work a spark, and both of them shall burn together, with none to quench it." "Wickedness burns like a fire." "You conceive chaff, you bring forth stubble; your breath is as a fire that will consume you" (Isa. 1:31; 9:18; 33:11. Compare 1:28). "To sin, wherever found, God is a consuming fire. If you choose sin, and refuse to separate from it, the presence of God, which consumes sin, must consume you." [12] Because of sin's destructiveness, Jesus purposes to free us from it.

"The religion of Christ means more than the forgiveness of sin; it means taking away our sins, and filling the vacuum with the graces of the Holy Spirit. . . . When Christ reigns in the soul, there is purity, freedom from sin." [13]

Out on our front lawn last fall and winter, one leafy tree stubbornly retained its faded leaves throughout the long winter. But with spring the sap began to flow. As it ascended the trunk and pushed out into every branch and tiniest twig, it crowded off the dead leaves which had clung to the tree throughout the long winter despite frost and storms. In the same way the Spirit works from within every willing person. When we give the Spirit full control of all dimensions of our being, He subdues and expels our sinful deeds, words, thoughts, and feelings; He transforms our natures. It is the Spirit—divine life from God within—that will deliver us from sin, when we submit all our choices to His guidance.

"The Christian's life is not a modification or improvement of the old, but a transformation of nature. There is a death to self and sin, and a new life altogether. This change can be brought about only by effectual working of the Holy Spirit."[14]

Paul says, "Be transformed by the renewal of your mind" (Rom. 12:2). The change will begin in our thinking, as we opt for the Christian privilege to control our thoughts, "and take every thought captive to obey Christ" (2 Cor. 10:5).

Children tend to execute a plan as soon as it occurs to them. Grown-ups usually consider the plan before they decide on its execution. So in our Christian growth our thinking patterns will change first, and in due time changes in lifestyle and character will follow. We ought to remember that "if the thoughts are not properly employed, religion cannot flourish in the soul."[15]

We can choose to be kept from sinning by the power of God through the Spirit. We are not computers, not programmed to act in a particular way. Every person is endowed with freedom of moral choice. This inestimable gift God gave to man at creation. Therefore, "No man without his own consent can be overcome by Satan. The tempter has no power to control the will or to force the soul to sin. He may distress, but he cannot contaminate."[16]

It is God's plan to vaccinate or immunize us against sin. Jesus can and will do this, just as most of us have been vaccinated against certain diseases. This He plans to do by filling us with the Spirit. "If His Spirit abides in the heart, sin cannot dwell there."[17] Being filled with the Spirit and to harbor sin are mutually exclusive. There is no room for sinful thoughts in the mind where the Spirit has full control. Jesus was thus vaccinated against sin. When temptations came and beat upon the door of His mind, they could not get inside because there was no room within. He was filled with the Spirit.

"By His obedience to all the commandments of God, Christ wrought out a redemption for man. This was not done by going out of Himself to another, but by taking humanity into Himself. Thus *Christ gave to humanity an existence out of Himself*. To bring humanity into Christ, to bring the fallen race into oneness with divinity, is the work of redemption. Christ took human nature that men might be one with Him . . . , that men may be partakers of the divine nature, and be complete in Him." [18] When we recognize our weakness, Jesus is willing and eager to take us into Himself that we might live His life. "Abundant grace has been provided that the believing soul may be kept free from sin; for all heaven, with its limitless resources, has been placed at our command." [19]

Through His sustaining grace Jesus through His Spirit aims to keep us from falling. The apostle Jude assures us of this by saying, "Now to the One who can keep you from falling and set you in the presence of his glory, jubilant and above reproach" (Jude 24, NEB).

God can and will, if we permit Him, keep us from falling into sin, just as anyone of us can keep a pencil standing on its sharpened tip, by holding on to its top. The pencil verily stands, but not by itself. God does not expect you and me to stand by our own strength or power. But He is willing and eager to hold us by His sustaining grace and keep us from falling. A person who stands through God's grace will do no boasting of sinlessness. He will take no glory or credit to himself, but will constantly praise God for His grace and goodness.

Since God has through the Spirit made available victorious living, He expects us to claim it. He has provided a wedding garment for everyone. If we refuse to accept it and persist in coming in our own sinful selves, we shall be like the man in the parable without a wedding garment (see Matt. 22:11-13). "By the wedding garment in the parable is represented the pure, spotless character which Christ's true followers will possess. . . . It is the righteousness of Christ, His own unblemished character, that through faith is imparted to all who receive Him as their personal Savior." [20]

The man without the wedding garment was thrown out from among the wedding guests. The same will be true of us if we refuse to be freed from our filthy garments of sin. "In the day of judgment the course of the man who has retained the frailty and imperfection of humanity will not be vindicated. For him there will be no place in heaven; he could not enjoy the perfection of the saints in light. He who has not sufficient faith in Christ to believe that He can keep him from sinning, has not the faith that will give him an entrance into the kingdom of God." [21]

God's plan for us is victory over temptation and deliverance from sin. But in spite of our committal to Christ, Satan will at times trip us. He is a wily foe. He knows that at times we can even become so preoccupied with doing good that we forget to be watchful of danger.

A chapel service was being conducted in one of our colleges before the time of air-conditioning. It was a warm spring day, and during the service the very high windows had to be opened. A student would usually walk down the outside aisle with his long pole with a hook on the end and would open window after window. Since they were close together, he would step from one to another without looking down on the floor. One of his classmates, noticing his friend's preoccupation, decided to play a trick on him by sticking his leg out into the aisle. His unsuspecting friend stumbled and fell, to the spontaneous glee of the other students.

In the same way Satan often trips us into sin. Therefore, Jesus said, "Watch and pray that you may not enter into temptation; the spirit indeed is willing, but the flesh is weak" (Matt. 26:41).

But even though we fall, we should not be heartbroken. God has not left us without help. The apostle John assures us, "My little children, I am writing this to you so that you may not sin; but if any one does sin, we have an advocate with the Father, Jesus Christ the righteous; and he is the expiation for our sins" (1 John 2:1, 2). If and when we stumble and fall, we should go to Jesus immediately and confess our sin, knowing that "if we confess our sin, he is just, and may be trusted to forgive our sins and cleanse us from every kind of wrong" (1 John 1:9, NEB).

When Satan reminds us of past failures, we may answer him in the words of the prophet Micah: "Rejoice not over me, O my enemy; when I fall, I shall rise; when I sit in darkness, the Lord will be alight to me" (Micah 7:8).

In spite of temporary setbacks and failures, God's original plan for every repentant sinner will be fulfilled. Men and women who have accepted His plan will be partakers of His glory and reflectors of His image. "By the power of the Holy Spirit the moral image of God is to be perfected in the character. We are to be wholly transformed into the likeness of Christ."[22] "The very image of God is to be reproduced in humanity. The honor of God, the honor of Christ, is involved in the perfection of the character of His people."[23] And when Jesus returns for His own, He will indeed "be glorified in his saints, and . . . be marveled at in all those who have believed" (2 Thess. 1:10).

---

[1] Ellen G. White, *Education*, p. 15.
[2] Ellen G. White, *Seventh-day Adventist Bible Commentary*, vol. 1, p. 1081.
[3] *Ibid.*
[4] *Ibid.*
[5] Ellen G. White, *Education*, p. 15.
[6] See Ellen G. White, *The Desire of Ages*, p. 161.
[7] See Ellen G. White, *The Story of Redemption*, p. 19.

[8] Ellen G. White, *Review and Herald,* Apr. 14, 1896.

[9] Ellen G. White, *The Great Controversy,* p. 505.

[10] Ellen G. White, *The Desire of Ages,* p. 32.

[11] Ellen G. White Comments, *Seventh-day Adventist Bible Commentary,* vol. 6, p. 1097.

[12] Ellen G. White, *Thoughts From the Mount of Blessing,* p. 62.

[13] Ellen G. White, *Christ's Object Lessons,* pp. 419, 420.

[14] Ellen G. White, *The Desire of Ages,* p. 172.

[15] Ellen G. White, *Counsels to Parents, Teachers, and Students* (Mountain View, Calif.: Pacific Press Pub. Assn., 1913), p. 544.

[16] Ellen G. White, *The Great Controversy,* p. 510.

[17] Ellen G. White, *Review and Herald,* Mar. 16, 1886.

[18] Ellen G. White Comments, *Seventh-day Adventist Bible Commentary,* vol. 7, p. 927.

[19] Ellen G. White, *Selected Messages,* bk. 1, p. 394.

[20] Ellen G. White, *Christ's Object Lessons,* p. 310.

[21] Ellen G. White, *Review and Herald,* Mar. 10, 1904.

[22] Ellen G. White, *Testimonies to Ministers,* p. 506.

[23] Ellen G. White, *The Desire of Ages,* p. 671.

CHAPTER 12

The Sin Against
the Holy Spirit

Of the sin against the Holy Spirit Jesus said: "Therefore I tell you, every sin and blasphemy will be forgiven men, but the blasphemy against the Spirit will not be forgiven" (Matt. 12:31). This is the mortal sin, or the sin unto death, that the apostle John speaks about in 1 John 5:16.

Of what does this dread sin consist for which there is no forgiveness? But possibly before we try to answer that question, it would be well to look at some instances recorded in the Bible where people committed the unpardonable sin, or sinned against the Holy Spirit.

Korah, Dathan, and Abiram, in rebelling against Moses and Aaron, committed the sin against the Holy Spirit (see Numbers 16). These three men stirred up and led a rebellion of 250 prominent men of Israel. They charged that Moses and Aaron had taken too much power to themselves. They insisted that they ought to share in ruling the people, since they thought they also had been called to leadership by God.

Moses did not try to vindicate himself. He left his case with God, and appealed to Him to settle the dispute (see Numbers 16:4 11). God made His verdict known by having the earth open up and swallow the three rebel leaders and their families (see verses 31 33). After that, fire came down from heaven and consumed their 250 followers (see verse 35).

Ellen White says that Korah, Dathan, and Abiram "had committed the sin against the Holy Spirit, a sin by which man's heart is effectually hardened against the influence of divine grace."[1] Obviously these rebels committed the unpardonable sin, since God Himself cut short their lives by blotting them out immediately.

Another illustration of sin against the Holy Spirit is found in the experience of Saul, the first king of Israel. After Samuel anointed him to be king, he was converted and received the anointing of the Holy Spirit. He became a new man (see 1 Samuel 10:6, 9). "A great change was wrought in him by the Holy Spirit. The light of divine purity and holiness shone in upon the darkness of the natural heart. He saw himself as he was before God. He saw the beauty of holiness."[2]

God Himself had called Saul to be king. He imbued him with the Holy Spirit (see 1 Sam. 10:6-10). Still the day came when Saul did not choose to follow God's biddings to destroy the Amalekite enemies of God (see 1 Sam. 15. Oh, yes, he obeyed partly, but not fully. He put his own ideas and will above God's plans. After a while the Holy Spirit left him (see 1 Sam. 16:14). Finally he went diametrically against God's command by consulting the witch at Endor (see Lev. 19:31; Deut. 18:10, 11) about the outcome of an imminent battle against the Philistines. Earlier in his reign he himself had ordered that all mediums and wizards be put to death throughout the whole land (see 1 Sam. 28:9). Saul, forsaken by God and defeated by the Philistines, died toward the end of the unsuccessful battle. He was eternally lost (see 1 Sam. 31). He had slighted "the reproofs and warnings of God's word or of His Spirit."[3]

Some people do the same today. They say they believe in God and His teachings. But since these do not agree with their ideas, they put their own notions and plans above God's counsel. King Saul did that very thing; and by doing so, he grieved away the Spirit of God and died eternally lost, although he once had been filled with the Spirit.

Attributing the work of the Spirit to Satan is another form of sin against the Spirit. This the scribes did when they attributed Jesus' exorcisms to Beelzebul (see Mark 3:22). Jesus warned them against this. "The Pharisees to whom Jesus spoke this warning did not themselves believe the charge they brought against Him. . . . They had heard the Spirit's voice in their own hearts declaring Him to be the Anointed of Israel, and urging them to confess themselves His disciples."[4] These men stifled the Spirit's promptings to them and sinned away their day of grace.

Lying to the Holy Spirit is another form of the mortal or unpardonable sin. Ananias and Sapphira, members of the early Jerusalem church, turned hypocrites and practiced fraud by telling Peter that they had sold their farm for the price they brought as an offering. By doing so "they lied to the Holy Spirit, and their sin was visited with swift and terrible judgment"[5] (see Acts 5:1-11).

By birth all of us are sinners. But it was sinners Jesus came to save. "The Son of man came to seek and to save the lost" (Luke 19:10). He draws human derelicts by the Spirit. He reached Mary Magdalene, even though she was a fallen woman stained with crimson sin. Through her response to the drawing of the Spirit "she became a partaker of the divine nature. The one who had fallen, and whose mind had been a habitation of demons, was brought very near to the Savior in fellowship and ministry."[6] It was Mary who lingered long at the cross (see Matt. 27:56). Mary helped at the burial of Jesus (see Matt. 27:61). She was first at the tomb on the resurrection morning (see Mark 16:1). Mary, who had been cleansed from her sins and washed whiter than snow in the blood of Jesus, was the first also to proclaim the risen Savior (see Mark 16:9, 10).

In His saving work, Jesus has never been deterred by a sinner's degradation, provided he is ready and willing to respond to His overtures of love through the Spirit. "He is able for all time to save those who draw near to God through him, since he always lives to make intercession for them" (Heb. 7:25).

The Spirit works with the unconverted. If He did not, no one would ever be drawn to Jesus in repentance for his sins. Jesus Himself said that the Spirit "will convince the world of sin" (John 16:8).

This ministry of the Spirit to unbelievers, called by theologians prevenient or common grace, the Spirit fulfilled on the Day of Pentecost. The listeners came "and said to Peter and the rest of the apostles, 'Brethren, what shall we do?' And Peter said to them, 'Repent, and be baptized every one of you in the name of Jesus Christ for the forgiveness of your sins; and you shall receive the gift of the Holy Spirit'" (Acts 2:37, 38). Praise the Lord! The sins of these visitors to the feast were blotted out.

But the sin against the Holy Spirit is unpardonable and results in eternal death. Many are puzzled over this unpardonable sin against the Spirit. They wonder what it really is. Some are afraid they have committed it and fear that they are eternally lost. But "no one need look upon the sin against the Holy Ghost as something mysterious and indefinable."[7]

From the four biblical incidents related above we learned that sin against the Holy Spirit may be committed in different ways. Korah, Dathan, and Abiram committed it through persistent resistance to God-appointed leaders; King Saul did it by insisting on having his own way, rather than following God's will for him; the Jewish leaders in the day of Jesus did it by attributing the work of God to the devil; and Ananias and Sapphira did it by lying.

In all these different ways, and others, we first grieve the Holy Spirit (see Eph. 4:30). As we persist in this attitude and action, we may even quench the Holy Spirit (see 1 Thess. 5:19). The unpardonable sin, or the sin against the Spirit, is persistent rejection of light. This inevitably blinds the spiritual eyes and hardens the rejecter's heart to the wooings of the Spirit. Finally there is utter darkness in the soul, and the person is eternally lost, because he has ruined his soul's receptivity to the promptings of the Spirit.

The sin that God never forgives is the sin that is never recognized, never abhorred, never repented of, and hence never forsaken. It will go down with the sinner to his grave and will bring eternal death. Ultimately it is the sin of self-will that often manifests itself in human pride and just plain selfishness. "The sin against the Holy Ghost is the sin of persistent refusal to respond to the invitation to repent."[8]

In trying to explain this to students in the classroom, I used to draw a picture of a big pit or well on the blackboard. At the bottom of that pit I placed a man. He could not possibly scale the sides and get out of the pit, but on the brim of the pit stood a man with a rope. He let the rope down to the man in the pit and asked him to take hold of it and tie it around his waist and then hold onto it while he and other men would pull him up. But even though the rope came down to him, the man at the bottom of the pit kept his hands stubbornly in his pockets, looked disdainfully at the rope, and ignored it. There was no help or salvation for him as long as he ignored the rope. He was offered help to be rescued from the pit, but he rejected the assistance by refusing to take hold of the rope. In the same way the Holy Spirit is trying to reach us; but if we refuse to respond to Him, there is no salvation for us. It is not God's will that we be lost. It is our fault.

The Holy Spirit wants to warm us and make us alive to the will of God, but we may quench His warming influence by putting, as it were, a wet rug over a burning candle. If we persistently refuse to walk in the light and continue to cherish the things that we know to be opposite God's will, we are on most dangerous ground.

To pray to God and continue to cherish an idol in our heart is blasphemy. God will set His face against such an individual (see Eze. 14:7, 8). If we do not clear out these idols, we will some day be "past feeling" (Eph. 4:19, KJV). No longer will we be able to hear the Spirit's voice or His call to repentance. Our prayer should be that of David in Psalm 19: "Keep back thy servant . . . from presumptuous sins; let them not have dominion over me! Then I shall be blameless, and innocent of great transgression" (verse 13). Presumptuous sins are those that we commit deliberately with wide-open eyes.

If we persist in going contrary to God's will and refuse to repent of our wrongdoing, we will ultimately come to the place where we will believe delusions. "Therefore God sends upon them [those who refuse the love of the truth] a strong delusion, to make them believe what is false, so that all may be condemned who did not believe the truth but had pleasure in unrighteousness" (2 Thess. 2:11, 12).

At times when I have stayed in a hotel away from home and have not had an alarm clock with me, I have asked the man at the desk to call me at a certain time in the morning. Imagine that after I had asked him to call me at 5:00 in the morning, I had taken the receiver off the hook. Five o'-clock would come and I would be solidly asleep, knowing nothing about the passing of the hours.

It is possible for you and me to break the connection with God by driving the Holy Spirit away from us so that He cannot convict us of sin. Without conviction there can be no repentance and hence no forgiveness. In that condition we will be eternally lost, because the Holy Spirit is God's only means of warning us and convicting us of sin. It is not that God is unwilling to forgive, but that He cannot reach us. We are like the man in the pit with the rope of rescue dangling beside him.

The Spirit is meek and humble. He does not hold a grudge. He is kind at all times. But He will not tolerate obstinate evil. I cannot act willfully and expect Him to stay with me forever. Such behavior will ultimately quench Him. If I am careless and thoughtless, this too may quench Him. I can do the same by being indifferent to Him.

I can quench the Spirit and silence the voice of God in my soul. It will be a dark night when the light goes out. For such a person there will be no morning. Only eternal separation from God—night.

It is not God's will for us that we perish. "The Lord is not slow about his promise as some count slowness, but is forbearing toward you, not wishing that any should perish, but that all should reach repentance" (2 Peter 3:9). The Old Testament prophet Ezekiel echoes the same divine purpose. "As I live, says the Lord God, I have no pleasure in the death of the wicked, but that the wicked turn from his way and live; turn back, turn back from your evil ways; for why will you die, O house of Israel?" (Eze. 33:11). Our Savior offers us all eternal life if we are connected with Him. When we are grafted into Him as into the vine, we partake of His life and His strength.

As there is no life for the branch if it is disconnected from the vine-stock, so there is no life for us if we persist in standing alone, apart from Jesus. We must choose to take hold of the rope that the Father and Christ are letting down into the pit of sin. That rope, or connecting link, is the Holy Spirit. Without our choosing to respond to His pleading invitation, we are eternally lost. If we resist His offer of rescue from the pit, we surely grieve all the Three Persons in the Godhead.

To accept salvation one must sense his need. Salvation is only for those who are poor in spirit, who are humble and contrite. "The Lord can do nothing toward the recovery of man until, convinced of his own weakness, and stripped of all self-sufficiency, he yields himself to the control of God."[9]

Man cannot initiate or generate a sorrow for sin. Jesus Himself told us what the work of the Holy Spirit is. He said: "When he is come, he will reprove the world of sin, and of righteousness, and of judgment: Of sin, because they believe not on me; of righteousness, because I go to my Father, and ye see me no more; of judgment, because the prince of this world is judged" (John 16:8-11, KJV). "Real sorrow for sin is the result of the working of the Holy Spirit."[10]

The Holy Spirit is to convict of sin. A man must be convicted of sin before he can repent. When a person has done something wrong, his conscience usually begins to hurt. He realizes his wrongdoing. It is the work of the Holy Spirit to prick his heart.

After an individual has been convicted of sin, he must repent. "Unless you repent you will all likewise perish" (Luke 13:5). A man must repent before God can forgive him. "Whom Christ pardons, He first makes penitent."[11] The sinner must be sorry for his wrongdoing and do his best to make things right. God will not pass over any sin that is not repented of, even though He is righteous and merciful; but He will forgive a confessed sin (see Prov. 28:13).

Someone must die for our sins. Either we ourselves will die ultimately in the lake of fire, or else Jesus died for us on the cross. The apostle Peter said: "Him hath God exalted with his right hand to be a Prince and a Saviour, for to give repentance to Israel, and forgiveness of sins" (Acts 5:31, KJV). Both repentance and forgiveness are gifts of God. "The goodness of God leadeth thee to repentance" (Rom. 2:4, KJV).

But we can commit the unpardonable sin in a more subtle way—simply by repeatedly yielding to the enemy's suggestion that we postpone our response to the promptings of the Spirit. I knew an individual who was a very good man. But his employment prevented him from easily accepting God's truth and becoming a member of the remnant church. He said that when he retired he would come all the way and accept God's truth and join the church. Finally the day came when he did retire, and he still did not accept God's plan for his life. He was a good, honest man; but he said, "It is impossible for me to give God now the remnants of my life." He reasoned, "I have lived all my life apart from Him, and it is kind of cowardly and unmanly to come to Him now when I will soon die." Thus he did not even then give his life to God.

We should remember that repeated actions form habits. Habits in turn make character. This individual had so long delayed or postponed giving his heart to the Lord that it became a habit and finally it became part of his character. It became impossible for him at the age of 65 or older to give his life to God. He had refused to do it so many other times that it became impossible for him to change his pattern of postponement. Satan knows that if he can prevail upon us only to postpone a decision for Christ over and over again, we will finally be his. We should remember that the decision not to make a decision for Christ is a decision for Satan by default. Many honest people are caught in this delusive trap by Satan. In this way too the Spirit may be quenched.

When a man refuses to respond to the goodness of God that is designed to lead unto repentance (see Rom. 2:4), his refusal to accept God's overtures of grace will result in the unpardonable sin and hence death.

---

[1] Ellen G. White, *Patriarchs and Prophets*, p. 405.
[2] *Ibid.*, pp. 610, 611.
[3] *Ibid.*, p. 635.
[4] Ellen G. White, *The Desire of Ages*, p. 322.
[5] Ellen G. White, *The Acts of the Apostles*, p. 72.
[6] Ellen G. White, *The Desire of Ages*, p. 568.
[7] Ellen G. White Comments, *Seventh-day Adventist Bible Commentary*, vol. 5, p. 1093.
[8] *Ibid.*
[9] Ellen G. White, *The Desire of Ages*, p. 300.
[10] *Ibid.*
[11] Ellen G. White, *Thoughts From the Mount of Blessing*, p. 7.

CHAPTER 13

A Spirit-filled People–
A Finished Work

To the eleven remaining disciples on Mount Olivet just before Jesus ascended to heaven, He said, "You shall receive power when the Holy
Spirit has come upon you" (Acts 1:8). The disciples received this promise
when they were about to assume the gospel commission. Soon after, they
were filled with the Spirit, and in the power of the Spirit they entered
upon their God-ordained work. The Spirit-filled apostolic church
preached for 30 years and evangelized the world. Every creature in the
then-known world heard the gospel within three decades (see Col. 1:23).

We have been preaching this message for more than a century and a
half, and still the task before us appears gargantuan. In Africa alone there are
millions of people who have never heard the name of Jesus Christ, much
less the advent message. While the church has begun to grow rapidly in
Asia, Africa, and elsewhere, the population is also exploding. One country,
India, has more than a million villages, besides numerous large towns and
immense cities. If Christ, while on earth, had begun to visit one Indian vil-
lage a day and continued to do so every day since, He would not finish visiting all the villages of India until sometime in the 2700s.

At present the population of the world is estimated at around six billion
and still increasing. If the world's population increased at, say a rate of 70-100
million a year, a number equal to the population of France, Belgium, and
Holland taken together is being added every year to the people living on this
earth, or a country almost as populous as China is superimposed upon the ex-
isting population of the world every decade. At such a growth rate the world
population would double in 38 years.[1]

From a human point of view I would say that, if we make no more
rapid progress in the future than we have made in he past, this work will
never be finished. But thanks be unto God, in spite of this, God's message

is continuously reaching a higher percentage of the world's population. In 1910 there was only one Seventh-day Adventist for every 13,600 people; in 1969, there was one for every 2200; but today there is approximately one for every 1430 people in the world. The population of the earth is increasing rapidly, but the church of God is growing faster.

Today the disciples' commission is ours. So is also the promise of the enabling power. This the messenger of the Lord confirms. "To us today, as verily as to the first disciples, the promise of the Spirit belongs. . . . At this very hour His Spirit and His grace are for all who need them and will take Him at His word."[2]

When we consider God's work throughout the earth, we should constantly remember this promise. The work will be finished by God and through His power. It is His work, and He assures us that "he will finish the work, and cut it short in righteousness" (Rom. 9:28, KJV). We—men and women—will never finish the work; God will finish it, but He will do so through us, provided we are willing to be instruments of His divine power.

As coworkers with God in finishing His work our supreme need as individuals and as a church is for the infilling of the fullness of the Holy Spirit and His accompanying power. Primarily we do not need more money. Money is good and convenient, but money is not indispensable. The disciples had none; they were imbued with the fullness of the Holy Spirit. We do not even need more and bigger institutions. Institutions will never finish the work; men and women, filled with the Spirit, will help God finish His work in the earth.

Certainly as a denomination we do not need a more structured organization. The organization of the Seventh-day Adventist Church encircles the globe and stretches its tentacles everywhere. It is the best system of organization possessed by any Protestant church. Neither do we primarily need higher education. It ill behooves me—one who has spent almost his entire service tenure in this denomination in our educational institutions—to depreciate the value of education or minimize the importance of scholastic learning. I know only that the indispensable fitness you and I need as members of the remnant church to make us mighty witnesses of Christ's saving power and His soon return in glory is not primarily scholastic learning; it is the infilling of the fullness of the Holy Spirit into our lives so that God through us might be enabled to utilize our present financial, institutional, organizational, and scholastic resources to their maximum.

About three decades ago one of the vice-presidents of the General Conference said that the Seventh-day Adventist denomination was a giant asleep. As a people with all our institutions and superb organization, we possess tremendous potential for efficient and speedy evangelization of the whole world. But the power of the Holy Spirit in His fullness is needed to make these resources achieve their fullest.

Napoleon is reported to have said, "China is a lion asleep. Do not awake her. When China is aroused she will change the face of the world." We who are now living have seen and are seeing the Chinese lion arousing.

A little over two decades ago the drowsy Chinese lion sleepily began to stir and began to exert an influence in international affairs. The People's Republic of China asserted her sovereign rights. Why do not Western nations move their armies into China today and tell her, as they did for centuries and during the Boxer Rebellion, what to do and how to do it? The European nations used to lead China by the nose through the political expediency of extraterritoriality, an indignity that no nation conscious of its power would tolerate. What has happened to China? Really nothing, except that today she has been filled with power through an infusion of the spirit of nationalism.

Today we—the church of God—need to be filled with power through the infilling of the Spirit of the living God. Without the Holy Spirit our efforts are of little avail. "It is the absence of the Spirit that makes the gospel ministry so powerless."[3] Everything, even the shed blood of Jesus Christ on Calvary's cross, is of no avail without the Holy Spirit.[4] We are living in the dispensation of the Holy Spirit.[5] But we do not seem to realize the power and the efficiency for service that might be ours by being filled with the Holy Spirit.

Moody had been preaching for years when an earnest yearning arose in his heart for the anointing of the Holy Spirit. He began to feel that he did not care to live unless he could receive this divine endowment for effective service. At that very time Chicago suffered a great fire, and Moody was sent to New York to solicit money for the rebuilding of the city. He was crying continuously for the infilling of the Holy Spirit. Here are his own words: "My heart was not in the work of begging. I could not appeal. I was crying all the time that God would fill me with His Spirit. Well, one day, in the city of New York—oh, what a day!—I cannot describe it; I seldom refer to it; it is almost too sacred an experience to name. Paul had an experience of which he never spoke for fourteen years. I can only say that God revealed Himself to me, and I had such an experience of His love that I had to ask Him to stay His hand. I went to preaching again. The sermons were not different; I did not present any new truths, and yet hundreds were converted. I would not now be placed back where I was before that blessed experience if you could give me all the world—it would be as the small dust of the balance."[6]

That was Moody's experience. "Why do we not hunger and thirst for the gift of the Spirit, since this is the means by which we are to receive power? . . . The presence of the Spirit with God's workers will give the presentation of the truth a power that not all the honor or glory of the world could give."[7]

God is waiting for His people to claim His promise—not merely be baptized with the Spirit, but to be Spirit-filled and Spirit-directed. And if we, as His people, are unwilling, He will find other means for the presentation of His last-day message. On His triumphal entry into Jerusalem, Jesus answered the Pharisees, when they requested Him to quiet the people who acclaimed Him as "the King who comes in the name of the Lord" (Luke 19:38), "I tell you, if these were silent, the very stones would cry out" (verse 40). If men and women refuse, babes, and even stones and rocks, will cry out His last message to the world.

God has used children before. During the advent awakening in the 1830s and early 1840s in Europe, the law prohibited anyone but ministers of the state church to preach in Sweden. Some, like Ole Boquist and Erik Walbom who tried, were imprisoned. Under these conditions the child preachers of Sweden arose to proclaim God's message for the hour.[8] If need be, God will do the same again. Or the stones will cry out.

God is not dependent on us. "God could have reached His object in saving sinners without our aid; but in order for us to develop a character like Christ's, we must share His work."[9] He *does* want to use us. And God forbid that He shall be compelled to find others to finish His work because of our unwillingness. But His people shall be willing in the day of His power (see Ps. 110:3). God is going to finish His work in the earth with men and women in the remnant church who are Spirit-filled and Spirit-directed.

The Holy Spirit is mentioned more often in Acts of the Apostles than in any other book in the Bible. Possibly this book could more appropriately have been called the Acts of the Holy Spirit, since the apostles and their fellow Christians, in doing their work for God, were only executing the directives of the Holy Spirit. They were filled with the Spirit and acted in accordance with the Spirit's biddings.

Philip ministered to the Ethiopian on the road to Gaza through the direction of the Spirit (see Acts 8:29). Peter went to Cornelius's house at the Spirit's order (see Acts 10:19, 20). The Council of Jerusalem framed policy "as it seems good to the Holy Spirit" (Acts 15:28). Paul was forbidden to enter Bithynia and turned toward Macedonia and Europe by the direction of the Spirit (see Acts 16:6-9). These are only a few instances where the Spirit directed. The book of Acts is the record of what the church accomplished under the minute guidance of the Spirit. The Spirit entered into the details of the work.

But the minute directions of the Holy Spirit did not safeguard the apostolic church from adversity and persecution. The book of Acts records the story of the triumphant onward march of the church amid adversities, persecution, and frequent imprisonments of the heralds of the gospel. Too often we forget the trials the church faced in apostolic times. As the Holy Spirit is mentioned more often in Acts than in any other book in the Bible, so are also more persecutions and imprisonments of the proclaimers of the gospel recorded in the book of Acts than in any other book of the Bible.

Possibly the story in Acts is to alert us to the conditions under which men and women, filled with the Spirit, will finish God's work in the earth. God's work will not be finished in tranquil times of peace and amid abundant material prosperity among God's people. Apparently such times and abundant means are no more conducive to the rapid spread of God's truth than are times of scarcity and suffering. God's work in the earth will be finished amid persecutions for His people.

The economic crisis coming upon the world will be such that all Seventh-day Adventists will be forced to make a clear-cut decision for or against God's will (see Rev. 13:11-17). All who then remain loyal to God will be glad to follow God's will for them in each minute detail, as did the Spirit-filled believers after Pentecost. All Adventists will then not only be baptized with the Spirit, but they will also be filled with the Spirit. Being filled with the Spirit, they will follow His promptings in everything, as did Mary when she anointed the feet of Jesus, even though she could give no reason for her act.

The final and climactic proclamation of God's truth before the imminent return of Jesus as King of kings and Lord of lords is symbolized by the third angel of Revelation 14 joined by the angel of Revelation 18. About the conditions then we read: "It is impossible to give any idea of the experience of the people of God who shall be alive upon the earth when celestial glory and a repetition of the persecutions of the past are blended. They will walk in the light proceeding from the throne of God. By means of the angels there will be constant communication between heaven and earth."[10] But the power of God is to be as mightily manifested in the remnant church as it was in the early church, so that no one will dare to join it unless his heart is right before God (see Acts 5:11, 13).

At that time God's people will not be "contending against flesh and blood, but against the principalities, against the powers, against the world rulers of this present darkness, against the spiritual hosts of wickedness in the heavenly places" (Eph. 6:12). But they will be filled with the Spirit through the latter rain in accordance with the prophet Zechariah's promise (see Zech. 10:1, KJV).

The terms rain, early rain, and latter rain are borrowed by the Hebrew writers from their agricultural seasons. The former or early rain fell in the seventh month, usually just after the Feast of Tabernacles. This corresponds to our fall or to September-October, but for the Israelites it was the season for the plowing of the fields and the sowing of barley and wheat. The early rain prepared the soil for the reception of the seed and its germination.

The latter rain fell shortly before the grain harvest and enabled the grain to fill out and ripen and prepare it for harvest. It fell about the end of the Jewish religious year, or roughly in March–April.

These terms, borrowed from the Palestinian agricultural seasons, are used by the Bible writers to symbolize great periods of spiritual refreshing in connection with the preaching of the gospel. "Near the close of earth's harvest, a special bestowal of spiritual grace is promised to prepare the church for the coming of the Son of man. This outpouring of the Spirit is likened to the falling of the latter rain." [11]

In the end-time the following promise will also be fulfilled: "The Holy Spirit, the representative of the Captain of the Lord's host, comes down to direct the battle. Our infirmities may be many, our sins and mistakes grievous; but the grace of God is for all who seek it with contrition. The power of Omnipotence is enlisted in behalf of those who trust in God." [12] Under the direction of the Captain of the Lord of hosts God's work in the earth will be finished in a blaze of glory. "During the loud cry, the church, aided by the providential interpositions of her exalted Lord, will diffuse the knowledge of salvation so abundantly that light will be communicated to every city and town. The earth will be filled with the knowledge of salvation. So abundantly will the renewing Spirit of God have crowned with success the intensely active agencies that the light of present truth will be seen flashing everywhere." [13]

Being filled with the Spirit, we shall be eager to follow His biddings. We shall welcome Him as did the disciples and their fellow believers on and after the Day of Pentecost and shall be repeatedly filled with Him as were the early

Christians. Even though temptations will assail us and we shall be threatened with death unless we renounce our loyalty to King Jesus, we shall not waver. We shall stand in the line of the heroes of faith spoken of in Heb. 11 of whom the apostle writes: "Women received their dead by resurrection. Some were tortured, refusing to accept release, that they might rise again to a better life. Others suffered mocking and scourging, and even chains and imprisonment. They were stoned, they were sawn in two, they were killed with the sword; they went about in skins of sheep and goats, destitute, afflicted, ill-treated— of whom the world was not worthy—wandering over deserts and mountains, and in dens and caves of the earth" (verses 35-38).

Like these heroes of faith, God's children in the sunset hours of earth's history will choose death rather than disobey God. They will make the same choice Jesus made: remain loyal to God at the cost of creature comforts and physical life. Like Luther before the Diet of Worms every one of them will then say: "I am a captive of the Word of God. I can do no other." They shall have so habituated themselves to do God's will that they cannot go contrary to it. It will be their very nature to follow Him.

When we as members of the remnant church submit fully to the guidance of the Spirit, we shall also begin to function as a unit under God's supreme direction. In a healthy state the five fingers on each hand function as a unit under the direction of the brain. I have a friend who was born with some nerves in one hand incorrectly connected. Therefore when he thinks he is bending one finger, another finger, contrary to his will, bends. All the fingers are not unitedly under the control of the brain. Consequently, they do not function as he wishes. When we as individuals in the church do not function as a unit under the biddings of God through the Spirit, but act independently, we act as the uncontrolled fingers on this man's hand.

The Holy Spirit is invisible, as is the wind. But as God was seen in Jesus, so the Spirit is to be seen in His church. As Christ was the image of the invisible God, so the church is designed to be the image of the now invisible Christ. The members of the church, transformed by the Spirit through the grace of Christ, will reflect the image of Jesus. In this way God will finish His work in the earth.

---

[1] Population experts believe that population growth is leveling off, but it will continue for some time.

[2] Ellen G. White, *Testimonies,* vol. 8, p. 20.

[3] *Ibid.,* p. 21.

[4] See Ellen G. White, *The Desire of Ages,* p. 671.

[5] See Ellen G. White, *Testimonies to Ministers,* pp. 511, 512.

[6] William R. Moody, *The Life of D. L. Moody* (New York: Fleming H. Revell Co., 1900), p. 149.

[7] Ellen G. White, *Testimonies,* vol. 8, p. 22.

[8] See LeRoy Edwin Froom, *The Prophetic Faith of Our Fathers* (Washington, D.C.: Review and Herald Pub. Assn., 1946), vol. 3, pp. 673, 674; Ellen G. White, *The Great Controversy,* pp. 366, 367.

[9] Ellen G. White, *The Desire of Ages,* p. 142.

[10] Ellen G. White, *Testimonies,* vol. 9, p. 16.

[11] Ellen G. White, *The Acts of the Apostles,* p. 55.

[12] Ellen G. White, *The Desire of Ages,* p. 352.

[13] Ellen G. White, *Evangelism,* p. 694.

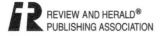

April 18   Intercession

- Sick
    - Pricille
    - Lillian
    - President's wife
    - Julie
    - she ick kids

- well being
    - Sadva
    - Dorothy
    - Brian
    - Jimmy
    - Daddy
    - Family

Petition

- Move dove to the thee o hr christ
- Work — Wisdom
            Knowledge
            Understanding

- Healing for my soul & my body.
- Remove Vanity oh Lord.

How do we reason with God

1. Prayer
   - groaning
   - Job's case
   - Jesus at Gethsemane
   - Jesus to the disciple
     you are servants

   • Let this middle
     in you
   • Ezek 36:28,)
   • Sheep metaphor
     "He leadeth me"

2. Bible study
   - God speaks to us

3. The Holy Spirit convicts us
   - of sin
   - of judgement to come.

   • Abraham
   • Zacharia
   • Moses

Confidence

> a child to a father
> and this is the confidence
  we have that when

A friend - Pierson's
   kid ad the bully